TRENDS IN WORLD ANTHROPOLOGY

About the Author

Lalita Prasad Vidyarthi (*b.* 1931) received his doctorate from the University of Chicago and is now Professor and Chairman of the Department of Anthropology at the University of Ranchi, India. Currently (1974-1978) he is the President of the International Union of Anthropological and Ethnological Sciences and of the 10th International Congress of Anthropological and Ethnological Sciences to be held in India in 1978. Dr. Vidyarthi is the President of the Indian Anthropological Association, a Founder-Member of the Indian Council of Social Sciences Research, Chairman of the Task Force on Development of Tribal Areas of the Planning Commission, and a Member of the Central Council on Tribal Research Institute of the Ministry of Home Affairs, Government of India. He is Founder-Editor of The Journal of Social Research, The Indian Anthropologist, and The Research Journal of Ranchi University. His major fields of research are the Tribal Culture of India including the Andaman and Nicobar Islands; Urban-Industrial political, and action Anthropology; Indian Civilization, the History of Indian Culture, Folklore, village studies and History of Anthropological Theories. He has to his credit several internationally popular books.

TRENDS IN WORLD ANTHROPOLOGY

L.P. VIDYARTHI

CONCEPT PUBLISHING COMPANY PVT. LTD.
NEW DELHI-110059

ISBN: 978-93-5594-194-7

Edition 2022

Published and Printed by

Concept
Since 1974

Concept Publishing Company Pvt. Ltd.
A/15-16, Commercial Block, Mohan Garden,
New Delhi-110059 (India)
T : 91-11-41101460
E : publishing@conceptpub.com, *W*: www.conceptpub.com

Contents

Introduction

THE book is somewhat enlarged form of a paper which I was invited to write by the International Social Science Council on the occasion of its Silver Jubilee celebration held in Paris in 1977. Along with me Prof. Fred Eggan was commissioned to review the development of Anthropology during the last one quarter of this century (1952-77), particularly in the USA, Great Britain, Africa and Latin America. Consequently my responsibility mainly focused on the study of the anthropological developments in Asian countries.

The Chapters that follow are based on both the literary sources and the field work. In reviewing the rise of Anthropology during the last quarter of this century the issues of *Current Anthropology* have been particularly helpful. As a matter of fact, the two volumes on *Anthropology Today* (A.L. Kroeber: 1953) and its *Appraisal* (Sol Tax: 1953) provided the base-line material while the issues of *Current Anthropology* in book form (William, Thomas: 1956) and in the form of journal, so ably edited by Sol Tax, have provided the material to understand the process of development and internationalization of Anthropology in different parts of the world. In addition a number of recent publications on anthropological theories such as Marvin Harris's Rise of Anthropological Theories (1968) and John J. Hanningman's Development of Anthropological Ideas (1976) were of immense help. The directories published by the Wenner Gren Foundation, the Annual Reviews of Anthropology, the International Bibliography of Social Sciences as well as periodical review papers and books have provided the background material to understand the anthropology of the last quarter century. A review of the proceedings of the World Congresses held during 1950-1975 (Vienna: 1952, Philadelphia: 1956, Paris : 1960, Moscow : 1964, Tokyo : 1968, Chicago : 1973) also helped me in assessing the trends in anthropological enquiries during the period under review. A survey of large number of research books on national and regional anthropology have further enabled me to understand the pattern of anthropological development in the different parts of the world.

My various visits to the different parts of the world since 1956 and my attendance in the World Congress gave me occasions to discuss the development in anthropology, particularly in the USSR, the European countries, Japan, Canada and the USA. Much as I wished, I could have no first hand information on anthropology in South Africa, Australia, South America and Oceania. However, my discussion with several scholars of these countries during Congresses and supportive reading have given me some insight into the understanding of the anthropological problems in these countries.

In the chapter that immediately follows, the emergence of American model in Anthropology during the period under review has been brought out. It is followed in brief by the contemporary anthropological theories which have influenced the anthropological thinking during the last quarter century. In this context of the infra-structural development of anthropology, has been studied European Anthropology with proper focus on the continuance of national Ethnography, in spite of Americanizing influence. The recognition of the evolutionary approach in the Soviet Union has also been discussed with first hand information.

The chapter that follows makes a detailed appraisal of the development of Anthropology in South Asia, particularly India. The same pattern of Americanizing influence is reflected in the study of Anthropology in South-East Asian countries and, of late, also in Japan. The analysis also informs how the American approach has, of late, been found short in bringing out the correct understanding of the anthropological scenes in the Asian countries.

In view of several constraints, particularly of time, resources and library facilities, the present review cannot claim to be exhaustive; rather it is illustrative of some of the manifold developments which a Third World Scholar could identify in course of his rapid review and research on the development of anthropology during the last 25 years.

While collecting and writing this book I was greatly benefited by the comments made available to me by a number of scholars, particularly Prof. M.N. Srinivas, Prof. Gopala Sarana, and Prof. Rabindra K. Jain.

The outline and some of the documents provided by Prof. Rokkan, the President of the I.S.S.C. provided a lot of insight in preparing this short volume, for which I am grateful to him.

I am particularly grateful to Mr. Asesh K. Haldar, who helped me immensely in preparing the manuscript and in handling the bibliographical details.

I am thankful to Sri Ram Autar Prasad who typed the materials repeatedly and prepared it for the press.

L.P. VIDYARTHI

1 The Emerging American Model in Anthropology

THE third quarter of the century opens in anthropology under the influence of A.L. Kroeber, the unquestioned chief of American Anthropology. He was one of the few practising general anthropologists in the profession to contribute with competence in ethnology, archaeology, linguistics and also in Physical Anthropology. In addition, he was an excellent summariser of his findings and implications in the study of man.

According to Kroeber, anthropology attempts to understand and inter-relate all principal aspects of mankind, with central emphasis on man's most distinctive product, namely, culture. The other social sciences are concerned with particular aspects of human culture : social, economic, political and personal. To him "the subject of anthropology is limited only by men, and, however specific it may often be in dealing with date, aims at being ultimately a co-ordinating science." (1953 : XIII-XIV) Examplified through his writings, under 532 titles, he established what he wrote in 1963.

"Anthropology alone was to deal with culture as such, both through total description and through conceptualization, theoretically. Associated with understanding of culture are knowledge of its past (prehistoric); of the most autonomous spatial sector of culture, namely, language; and even of the racial physics and bodies of men that have produced culture

(Physical Anthropology). The first two of these associated studies—archaeology and linguistics—are usually considered humanities, when pursued in isolation; analogously racial and ropology is obviously also part of biology. No other social science allows its operation to extend so far into frankly humanistic or natural science. This anomaly of anthropology is undoubtedly connected with its other anomalous feature in the social sciences, its holistic instead of segmental interest of culture." (Kroeber :1963 : 161).

Thus, the interaction of anthropology with biological sciences, on the one hand, and humanistic and social sciences, on the other, is quite evident. The American traditions in anthropology which have accelerated the processes of the World Anthropology continued to percolate during the last quarter century and Anthropology extended its horizon in terms of theory, methods and substantive studies to an integrated understanding of man.

The other model of integration was proposed by the British anthropologists, particularly by Radcliffe-Brown who talked about a natural science of society keeping the biological and humanistic man out of focus. The functional and structural school of the British Social Anthropology emphasised the study of social systems, and endeavoured to develop a unified science of society inclusive of Economics, Sociology, Psychology, Political Science, etc. In course of his lectures (now published in book form: Radcliffe-Brown : 1948, 1957). Radcliffe-Brown maintains that there can be only one science of society :

> One of the theses I am maintaining is that if it is possible that there shall be a science of society, there shall be only one such science. I am maintaining that we cannot have an independent science of law, of economics, of politics, etc., that insofar as such sciences are theoretical as distinguished from practical science, they must be part of a single general science of society. I admit that it can have a practical management, etc. That is perfectly true. I am maintaining the thesis that if there is to be a theoretical science of society in which we are seeking directly for

natural laws, then there can be only one theoretical science of human society.

These two major models of Anthropology, along with the European concept of Ethnology (reference to which will be made later) continued to compete with each other, for recognition and acceptance during the last quarter century.

In 1952, when the historic International Symposium was organized by Wenner Gren Foundation of Anthropological Research under the chairmanship of A.L. Kroeber, the American Model of anthropology found better recognition, and received a systematic exposure to international community of anthropologists. In his introductory remarks, Kroeber observes emphatically :

> After all, the subject of Anthropology is limited only by man. It is not restricted by time—it goes back into geology as far as men can be traced. It is not restricted by region but is world-wide in scope. It has specialized on the primitives because no other science would deal seriously with them, but it has never renounced its intent to understand the higher civilisations also. (A.L. Kroeber : 1953, XII)

In general, an appraisal of both the volumes 2 (A.L. Kroeber : 1953, and Sol Tax *et al* : 1953) goes to define and defend the status of anthropology as a 'co-ordinating holistic and integrative science', as special bodies of international knowledge about man, 'flowing out of man, centred in him, product of him.'

This American view of Anthropology decidedly found all round recognition. In the symposium and among many, Levi-Strauss went to say that—"in most cases the so-called social sciences are not sciences at all." He found the social science approach lacking in depth while both the humanities and the nature sciences work at a deep level. To quote him :

> We all agree that anthropology has a close relationship with the humanities, the social sciences, and the natural sciences. Another point of view is that of the depth at

> which those sciences work. It seems to me that both the humanities and the natural sciences work at a deep level, while so far, social sciences remain quite on the surface level in most cases the 'social sciences' are not sciences at all. They are rather acts that are trying to use the very little we know about social phenomenon for a better kind of living . . . Anthropology tries to jump to a deep level, while social sciences have been so far unable to do so, and the result is an extremely difficult situation for co-operation between anthropology and the social sciences. This should be the first problem to overcome. (1953 : 154)

In course of the discussion, Mead further clarifies Levi-Strauss's stand and amplifies his statement. She observes :

> Anthropology uses method of analysis from different levels (embryology, geology) with different units and different time scales, cross-cutting all disciplines relating man to nature, on the one hand, and in history, on the other, while sociology is an analysis on a single level, leaving psychological and biological analysis to other disciplines. (Mead : 1953 : 54)

The integrated image of Anthropology which emerges from the 1952 symposium and its approaches for studying the 'integrated' man was further followed up by the publication of the book entitled *Current Anthropology* (William L. Thomas : 1956). With the review papers on the various branches of anthropology as well as of the important theories, this book on anthropology updated the picture originally presented in *Anthropology Today* in 1952. Though among reviewers, the book had a better representation of British social anthropologists and European ethnologists, in the two concluding papers, the same thesis regarding the integration of anthropology was further reinforced by Sol Tax and A.L. Kroeber. In this paper Kroeber took note of the formation of the Institute of Social Relation at Harvard University with their stronger union with sociology. However, he overlooked this trend as an isolated example in the United States (1956 : 308).

The American anthropology further distinguished itself

by initiating the publication of *Current Anthropology*, a world journal of the science of man since 1959. It, further, carried the spirit of integration in Anthropology as it continued to publish papers from all over the world on prehistory, archaeology, linguistics, folklore, ethnology, social anthropology and physical anthropology.

Through the manifold innovative devices of its Editor Sol Tax, *Current Anthropology* facilitated inter-communication among the students of Man, all over the world. Again, through it, scholars could publish and read more promptly, and the whole range of material could appear in units small enough to be easily handled.

Current Anthropology was made available to its associates all over the world at a rather very concessional rate. By its policy it published review papers on theory, methods, ethnography and national anthropological styles from different parts of the world. Working with a democratic spirit, it first consolidated American anthropology and then radiated its scholarship, skill and ideas to the rest of the world. It also published material about anthropology and anthropologists in other parts of the world. These efforts led to the worlds and thus helped the internationalization of the discipline. It tried also to win over, though in fraction, the language barriers by publishing materials in English, originally written in their respective national languages.

The American dominance and internationalization of American brand of Anthropology during this quarter century is also reflected in its successful efforts to organize the two international congresses of Anthropological and Ethnological Sciences in 1956 in Philadelphia and 1973 in Chicago. The Fifth International Congress, in Philadelphia, in addition to receiving delegates from different countries, for the first time was attended by a delegation from the Soviet Union. It marked the entry of Soviet Anthropology into the World Anthropology in a big way, which further prepared ground for holding the Seventh Congress of Anthropological and Ethnological Sciences in Moscow in 1964. The Ninth Congress, again, held in Chicago confirms the influence of Sol Tax in American Anthropology. This Congress, unique and vast in its organization has been instrumental in generating the publication of a large number of volumes under the series, World Anthropology. Out of the two thousand papers received for the Congress, 360 papers (i.e. 18% of them) were received from the Third World countries, while the large majority of the congress papers (82%) were by the scholars identified with the industrialized world which fathered our discipline and nursed the career of the Congress itself. Such a goal to ensure better participation by the Third World scholars was fixed by Sol Tax. In his Preface to the volumes of World Anthropology, he observes : "These 360 papers are more than the total of all papers published after the last International Congress of Anthropological and Ethnological Sciences which was held in Philadelphia in 1956." (Sol Tax : 1975B, 7)

The dominance of American anthropology further gets reflected if one makes a demographic study of institutions and publication in Anthropology as revealed in the international directories and also the international bibliographies of anthropology, respectively. The original International Directory of Anthropologists was published by the National Research Council, Washington, D.C., in 1938 edited by an American scholar, Alfred Vincent Kidder. It presents a picture of anthropology immediately before the second world war. A revised version of this directory was published in 1940. Prof. M.J. Herskovits, another American Professor edited the third Directory which gave a picture of anthropology during the second world war. Finally, Sol Tax, the then editor of *Current Anthropology*, edited the fourth (1967) and the fifth (1975B) international directories.

An appraisal of the fifth directory, which is evidently very comprehensive, presents certain interesting facts. It brings out, on the one hand, the dominance of American anthropology, and on the other, the emergence of anthropology in the Third World countries where anthropology was unknown in 1938 (Table No. 2, P.VIII of *Fifth International Directory of Anthropologists*). According to this Directory, out of 4,765 registered anthropologists about half were from the USA and Canada, one-fourth from Europe (Western Europe 899, Eastern Europe 324) and only the remaining one-fourth hailed from the Third World, the chief countries of anthropological enquiries (Latin America 246, Western Asia 56, Africa 115,

South and South-East Asia 215, Far East 224, Oceania 129). It is quite likely that some anthropologists have failed to be included in the directory but their number, according to Sol Tax, will not exceed 760 proportionate to the figures of anthropologists of the countries actually entered in the directory. The distribution of anthropologists thus, has remained centered in the North Atlantic industrial countries.

Along with the anthropologists the anthropological institutions are equally unevenly distributed : 110 in New York, 78 in Chicago, 52 in Washington, 47 in Los Angeles, 45 in Philadelphia, 111 in the USA, 52 in London, 99 in Paris, 70 in Tokyo, while in other Third World countries the number at one place does not exceed 15, highest being 14, each in Calcutta and Delhi (Sol Tax : 1975 : 484-494).

Viewed in terms of their interests in the area of study (chronological index) we note the highest interest of the anthropologists has been recorded in contemporary time (3,315), and the second two highest being in the ethnographic present (2,185) and the historic time (2,127). Among the prehistoric times, the Neolithic Age appears to be more popular with 1,103 listing, followed by the Palaeolithic Age (868), the Bronze Age (311) and Iron Age (200). (Sol Tax : 1975B : 449-456)

The subject index for cultural anthropology tabulated in the directory brings out several interesting and useful indices reflecting the extent of interests of cultural anthropologists in its different sub-fields and themes. Some of the traditional categories like economic anthropology (663), kinship and marriage (513), social structure and social organization (822), tribal groups (764) and ethnography (355) have turned out to be major categories in which large number of anthropologists continued to be interested. Again, there are certain new fields in anthropology which have attracted large number of cultural anthropologists. These are : ecological anthropology (432), development and modernization (471), community studies (366), anthropology of education; theoretical and applied anthropology (224), anthropology of art and aesthetics (309), medical anthropology (260), political anthropology including administration (489), urban anthropology (392), social cultural and economic change (868), complex societies (204), etc. There are certain extremely new features, specially in the field of theory and method which have emerged as new fields of investigation. Among these emerging areas mention may be made of Symbolic Anthropology and symbolism (119), structuralism and Structural Anthropology (78), statistics, computers and mathematical model (80), systems analysis, systems theory and cybernetics (19), world views (40), history and sociology of knowledge (80), population and demography (184), culture of poverty (31), ethno-psychology and ethno-psychiatry (22) and Ethics in Anthropology and Ethnography (50). These persisting areas of inquiry as identified from the directory will be pursued in course of our discussion later. However, from a general perusal of the directory data, the overwhelming influence of the Anglo-Saxon scholars is quite obvious.

The uneven distribution of anthropologists can also be examined in the light of the geographical areas of their publication. A count of their publication on certain selected topics of cultural anthropology from the *International Bibliography of Anthropology* (Vol. XX, 1974) is given in Appendix 1. From this exercise it is evident that though the native anthropologists of African, Asian and Pacific countries are the least, publications on these countries are the maximum. For example, in that particular year, the total publications on five selected topics (ethnography, social structure, religion, folk literature, acculturation and social change) comes to 118 books and 133 papers which compare well with USA with 113 books and 169 papers. So are the figures for Asia and Oceania in comparisons to USA and Europe. (Rupp. Britter : 1976).

Along with the internationalization of anthropological literature through the publications of world journal of anthropology, through international symposia and through promoting bibliographical sciences as media of international communication, the third quarter of the present century has also witnessed the exchange of scholars on a large scale, for the purposes of studies, lectures and field researches. The support of the American foundations opened doors for such exchanges between America and other friendly countries of the world. Among such foundations that promoted large scale exchange of scholars on global plane, mention may be made of Fulbright

Smithmundt Programme, Rockfeller and Ford Foundations, the Wenner Gren Foundation for Anthropological Research, foreign-area research programmes of several universities, associations and institutes including the Smithsonian Institute.

Under the Fulbright programmes alone, for example, a large number of scholars were exchanged between America and India. Even in the early period of Indo-American programmes (1950-1964) 10 Indian anthropologists and 37 sociologists came to America and 13 anthropologists and 17 sociologists from America came to India under this programme. During this period (1950-63), 125 Americans came to India in the American Institute of Indian Studies. Later, the number went up, though in India in the 'seventies, it sustained a set back (*Fulbright Newsletter*, 1964).

Anthropology in the western and industrial countries was mainly concentrated around the colonial and developing countries. In order to support this approach a large part of their curriculum dealt with the ethnography and related museums on 'other culture' or countries of specialization. This approach received additional strength in America after 1945, when there was a rapid rise in the interest for non-American area courses. This tradition culminated in the development of the curriculum on area study programme on many campuses. Anthropology along with other disciplines received considerable funds for this purpose and, as a result, many anthropology departments strengthened their teaching and research activities on diverse regions of the world. Today, therefore, one finds strong and comprehensive programmes on Africa at such institutions as California at Los Angeles, Wisconsin, Michigan State, North Western of Evanston, Syracuse and at Indiana; on Europe at Harvard, Columbia and Massachusetts; on Asia at Cornell, Michigan, Standard, Pennsylvania, Chicago and Harvard; on the Arctic at Wisconsin; on Latin America, Florida, Arizona, Columbia, Illinois and John Hopkins on Oceania at Yale, Oregan, Hawaii, Cornell, Washington (Seattle) and Stanford. (C. Frantz : 1975)

Similar foreign area programmes were organized in the mid-'fifties, and 'sixties in the neighbouring country of Canada, though on a limited scale. The National Academy of Sciences of U.S.S.R. also realized the importance of such area-based researches and several scholars were trained to work on certain areas, particularly Africa, South and South-East Asia, Arctic region, South America and Europe in several centres, including the Institute of Ethnography, located at Moscow and Leningrad. The area-studies in the U.S. and Canadian institutions include both library and field work. In the case of the U.S.S.R., because of obvious limitations, the field-work based area-research remains to be minimal.

Taken together, then, the third quarter of this century has witnessed phenomenal developments in the fields of internationalization of anthropology. This internationalization mainly meant the flow of skill, resources and other impetus from America to the rest of the world. Prior to the 'fifties and also prior to the second world war, the British anthropology had its strong-hold in her Commonwealth countries. The Dutch and the French followed them in promoting colonial anthropological interests.

With the increasing American influence, the attitude of native anthropologists in the colonial countries underwent some radical change. In the second quarter of this century, for example, there was almost complete acceptance of the British traditions in Indian Anthropology. The Indian nationals educated at Cambridge, Oxford, London carried on with pride the great traditions of British Anthropology as reflected in their studies of tribal ethnography, kinship system, cultural contracts, social organization, etc. With the Americanising influence, the new trends such as, the village studies, the urban and industrial studies, the study of power structure and leadership, the study of complex societies and action research, etc. were introduced. Initially those who were educated at Oxford or Cambridge or London and who were in key positions at Indian Universities and in government service were skeptical about what American scholarship had to offer. This attitude was so generalized that even the young scholars who were selected for higher studies in the USA under the Fulbright and Smithmundt Programme (established in 1950) were ambivalent to the United States and to the American approach (M.S. Gore : N.D.). To some it is a form of informal imperialism, or neo-colonialism in other words. American trends reflect a type of inter-group domination in which formal administrative controls are absent and influences are canalized through the locally linked and other informal sources.

To conclude then, the period under review has witnessed phenomenal development of institutions, forums, foundations and media of communications, particularly at the American sources which have accelerated the tempo of internationalization of anthropology. The International Union of Anthropology and Ethnological Sciences affiliated to International symposia organized either by the Wenner Gren Foundation or by the financial assistance of the Ford and Rockfeller Foundations have helped in this process. With the decline of colonial anthropology of the British, Dutch and French brands, the Americanizing influence in anthropology have almost enjoyed a monopoly.

2 | Contemporary Theories and their Internationalization

ANTHROPOLOGY aims at understanding man and his culture. For this purpose, it has endeavoured, in the course of its history, to discover a set of theories and related methods. These theories originated and developed in Europe and then in America, and later spread in other parts of the world. While these theories and methods have undergone considerable modification and revision, and new ones have been added, the major ideas underlying them have never become obsolete. In the present context it will be my endeavour to refer to them in their proper historical context, and to emphasise and understand their status during the third quarter of this century.

Cultural Evolutionism

There is no denying the fact that anthropology began as a science of history. This historical interest of man to know about his origin and development dates back to ancient scholarship of Greece, Rome, China and India. The ancient thinkers made early reconstructions of remote cultural origin and development, though these were not based on any archaeological or other evidence of the past.

In the mid-nineteenth century when anthropology was growing up as a discipline the same historical question of origin and evolution irritated the classical evolutionists like Darwin, Morgan and Tylor. Even their critic, Wilhelm Schmidt proposed a more empirical method of historical ethnology. Durkhiem and his associates struggled to escape from the theoretical sterility of evolutionism by means of a primarily synchronic type of sociological analysis, yet they also occasionally succumbed to speculating about cultural origins and developments.

In spite of its historicity, necessity and comprehensiveness, the theory of evolution was severely criticized, and practically abandoned by all the Anglo-Saxon scholars from late nineteenth century to almost mid-twentieth century, as it got closely linked up with Karl Marx, and Fredrick Engels and their interpretations of society. The American cultural anthropologists like Robert Lowie labelled the later half of the nineteenth century as a period of 'evolutionary schematism', and in his book (Lowie : 1937) he completely avoided dealing with Karl Marx and Fredrick Engels who took greater pains in explaining historical change in theoretical terms than in setting up stages of cultural evolution. This position was later corrected by Marvin Harris in his book published in 1968 (Harris : 1968).

While most of the American and British anthropologists, till the 'fifties of this century, were mostly ignoring the theory of cultural evolutionism, Leslie White and in some ways Julian Steward and George Peter Murdock made efforts to revive evolutionary interests in the name of neo-evolutionism. The British archaeologist Gordon Childe provided the archaeological base to prove the stages of development proposed by Morgan and Tylor, and thus joined Leslie White in the post-war emphasis on the technological factor and use of the Marxist theory.

Julian Steward (1955) endeavoured to study evolution as a process of ecological adaptation, and identified the sequences of development in terms of cross-cultural regularities in limited areas. It was rather a partial acceptance of the postulates of the nineteenth century evolutionism.

Gordon Childe (1942, 1951) and Leslie White (1949) while emphasising the technological factor, visualised culture in global terms and put forth numerous scientific explanations and evidences in support of the unilinear or universal evolution.

When the American anthropologists were holding aloof from cultural evolution, Murdock, as early as 1949, examined kin terms in the evolutionary perspective and proposed what is termed as the 'main sequence theory'. Elman R. Service, a member of the next anthropological generation lends his support to cultural evolution. He, however, refuses to accept one single factor in culture as the prime mover in cultural development (1962 : 36, 102). In a concept very similar to that of Steward, Service defines evolution as an adaptive process involving the selection of new or the adjustment of the old cultural traits of a society for the society to improve its chances of survival, security and growth.

The influence of the evolutionary theory of the nineteenth century, however, was greatly recognised in the U.S.S.R. and other socialist countries. The Soviet Ethnography, as a matter of fact, developed on the lines indicated by evolutionary theory, and was further modified by the writings of Marx, Engels and Lenin. Referring to such researches, the Soviet ethnographers Bromley and Kozlov observe :

> Methodologically, research into national processes is based on the works of Lenin particularly on his concept of the two tendencies in the national problems and the laws governing the evolution of nation and international religion. (Y.V. Bromley and V.J. Kozlov : 1974 : 118)

Supporting the theory of neo-evolutionism of Russian brand, another Soviet scholar and Editor of *Soviet Ethnography*, Y.V. Averkiyeva observes :

> Beginning with the 1950s we observe a feverish search for a 'theory of development', in fact, even an 'anthropology of development' emerged. By the end of 1950 this search took the form of 'renaissance of evolutionism', vividly expressed in connection with the centenary of the publication of Darwin's *Origin of Species*, when, as Julian Steward, the well-known U.S. anthropologist, described it, there was a 'universal proclamation', of evaluationism. (Averkiyeva : 1974 : 312)

The review and reinterpretation of neo-evolutionism to understand class societies constitutes quite a significant development in the contemporary anthropological theories. It is also a pointer to the recognition of once hated theories on international level. Marvin Harris terms this approach as 'neo-cultural materialism', which is a sort of synthesis of the ideas of neo-evolutionism and improved Marxism. (Harris, Marvin : 1968)

In the context of the study of social change and to explain the social routes of contemporary revolutionary movements, Little admits that "anthropologists must now read with equal attention Durkhiem, Marx, Merton, Pareto as well as Firth, Linton, Lowie, Malinowski, Radcliffe-Brown" (K. Little: 1963: 336). In a recent paper, Firth deplores the unfortunate neglect of the contribution of Marx to neo-evolutionism which helps in understanding the class society.

Levi-Strauss, in his paper "Anthropology : its Achievements and Future" also lends support to unilinear evolution and disapproves of the concept of cultural relativism. He observes :

> The doctrine of cultural relativism is deemed unacceptable by the very people on whose behalf it was upheld, while those ethnologists who favour unilinear evolutionism find unexpected support from people who desire nothing more than to look at themselves as temporarily backward rather than permanently different. (C. Levi-Strauss : 1966 : 125)

The cultural relativity theory emphasising 'particularism' in culture was developed by American anthropologists (Melville J. Herskovits: 1955, 1956). This theorysustained a setback with the revival of neo-evolutionism. Even some of the American scholars found it uncomfortable to accept it. Redfield was one of earlier American anthropologists to realise the danger in supporting cultural relativism. He was strongly of the opinion that "the doctrine of ethical neutrality and 'benevolent' attitude of scientists to all variants of value system cannot be accepted for it would mean an equally benevolent attitude to the value system of the colonial peoples and to the value system of the Nazis." (R. Redfield : 1953 : 145-146)

In many of their writings the Soviet ethnologists bitterly questioned the foundation of the concept of cultural relativism as "it enhances the ideology of racialism." (Y.V. Averkiyeva : 1959, 1974) Averkiyeva considers it "particularly reactionary both in the theory and in the practice of international relations." (1974 : 315)

In initiation of such a dialogue, as far as I remember, goes back to 1956, when the Soviet scholars came to attend the Vth International Congress of Anthropological and Ethnological Sciences at Philadelphia, and had direct confrontation with the supporters of cultural relativity theory, especially M. Herskovits. The culmination of this process of intellectual interactions between Soviet scholars and others was reached when the VIIth International Congress of Anthropological and Ethnological Sciences met in Moscow in 1964 and Soviet ethnographers got a chance to demonstrate their science to the world. In this Congress, the most distinguished figure was American scholar, Leslie White, who was unfortunately ignored in the Western World owing to his commitment to evolutionary school. The *Current Anthropology* could also stimulate the intellectual contacts which enabled the Soviet and non-Soviet scholars to interact on the international level, and thus learn from each other in the fields of anthropological theories and methods.

Diffusion, Culture Area and Innovation

If classical evolutionism has survived the onslaught of time, and now has led to manifold areas of analysis, classical diffusionism has exposed its weak premises, and has almost been led to rest. Historically the British diffusionism founded by W.H.R. Rivers, Elliot Smith and W.J. Perry and the German diffusionism led by Ratzel and Graebner, Wilhelm Schmidt and few other Catholic fathers, became as Marvin Harris puts it, 'palpably bankrupt by mid-century'. "They require our attention, however, today only as an evidence of the tide that was running against nomothetic principles." (Harris : 1968) The use of the concept of diffusion in understanding cultural history, according to Koppers (Wilhelm Koppers : 1956 : 169-181) has been used by McCarthy (Frederick D.

McCarthy : 1953), Hodgen (Margaret T. Hodgen : 1950, 1952) and Robert Heine-Geldern (1954, 1955) and several others in the recent times.

Recently a movement of 'New Diffusionism' has been initiated by a group of British anthropologists. A quarterly journal, *The New Diffusionist*, is being edited by C.E. Joel since 1971. A perusal of the papers published in these issues reflects their interest (*i*) to bring diffusionist approach and concept up to date, (*ii*) to subject them to critical analysis in the light of advances in Anthropology and Archaeology, and (*iii*) to restore historical perspective in all fields of Social and Cultural Anthropology.

In the United States, diffusionists' thinking remained confined to the concept of 'culture area', *i.e.* relatively small geographical unit based on the contiguous distribution of the cultural elements. The theory initiated by Boas and followed by Wissler (1917) found its final refinement when Kroeber defined these concepts more sharply (A.L. Kroeber : 1939).

In India, Nirmal Kumar Bose was greatly influenced by Kroeber and Wissler's trait-distribution studies. Three of his important research fields : viz. Spring Festival Culture Complex (1927), Indian Temple Architecture (1949) and Survey of Material Culture in India (1961) were greatly influenced by American diffusionism.

In the turn of this quarter of the century, however, the concept of diffusion got linked up with the interpretation of short-range history and acculturation theory. The large scale modernization process initiated in the developing countries linked the concept of diffusion with innovation on the one hand, and their acceptance on the other. Homer G. Barnett, for example, studied the entire anthropological implications of innovation in the Trust Territory of the Pacific Islands (Barnett : 1953). Barnett's research generated new interest in communication research, as he linked the rate and transmission of innovation to socio-psychological factors prevailing in the society. International assistance by Western countries for the purpose of furthering economic development and the modernization of agriculture, public health or other adaptive activities in the under-developed lands attracted large number of social scientists including anthropologists. It provided an opportunity to develop and to make practical use of the theory of culture, and their ethnographic skill for a humanitarian purpose. The western (particularly American) anthropological skill, thus, got internationalized during the 'fifties.

Such indiscriminate introduction of innovations with unpleasant ethnocentric overtones also brought a change in the attitude of the developing communities. They also felt that a change along the western line was less preferable to the traditional ways.

The Functional, Structural and Integrational Schools

The functional-structural school which emerged as the most dominant school during the 'thirties of this century, owes its origin to two factors : first, a reaction to the historical schools of Anthropology and second, to the stimulation of French sociological school led by Durkheim. The fundamental theoretical premises of British social anthropology led by Malinowski and Radcliffe-Brown and followed by their large number of pupils are based upon Durkheim's concept of social solidarity. The sociological premises prosposed by Durkheim were evidently supported by the unique quality of their field researches which had been of a quite unprecedented intensity. No professional had ever before spent two full years studying a single tribal group, actually living in a native village and sharing the native way of life. This anthropological tradition of intensive and extended field work was definitely a greater contrast to the distributional researches of the cultural fossils or the traits. The functional-structural theory, again, emphasised on the study of a society as a sub-system within a single system.

Taken together, as a contrast to the two historical schools, the functional-structural school led an empirical, scientific and synchronic analysis of limited units. In spite of their emphasis on synchronic approach, they did recommend and made diachronic studies wherever reliable documents, archaeological and other evidences were available. The functional-structural trend of British social anthropology, by the late 1930s had gained virtually unchallenged control of the anthropological establishment throughout the British empire. Between 1930 and 1955, the overwhelming bulk of the contributions of the structural-functional school was based upon field work in African tribal societies located in the European, specially British, occupied territories.

In a review of functional approach, Raymond Firth brings out the strength of functional analysis and asserts that "in a very real sense it can be said that all British social anthropologists today are functionalist." (Firth : 1955 : 247) His observation further finds support from Fortes when he calmly claims that functional anthropology is "the generally accepted basis of theory and research in British social anthropology." (Fortes : 1953 : 18-27)

The British social anthropology with its overtone of functional-structural approach has been instrumental in reinforcing its relationship with modern sociology dominated by Talcott Parsons and Merton who regard the concept of function as a valuable tool of analysis. Such a trend, which may be termed as social science approach, also found its re-inforcement in a symposium held in Cambridge in June 1963 and the publication of its proceedings in four valumes. (Michael Banton : 1965, 1966). It was rather an effort of the British social anthropologists for a new lease of life as their old fields of study of 'other cultures' in their colonies were gone. Their senior colleague, Edmund Leach also started rethinking about Anthropology (Leach : 1961) but since most of the senior social anthropologists have retired from the field of study, it is to see what direction the British social anthropology takes. As the trend indicates, by and large they look to Levi-Strauss for intellectual stimulation, as Radcliffe-Brown did in the 'twenties, to draw leads from Durkheim, though they worked under the British teachers. In some decolonized countries including India, the persisting impact of British anthropology is so great that, with this recent move, some of them refuse to make distinction between Sociology and Social Anthropology.

During the 1940s and early 1950s, Radcliffe-Brown's social structural theory proved widely influential in several parts of the world, including North America. In America, however, the structural-functional school underwent modification and achieved a brilliant synthesis with American historical particularistic approaches when Radcliffe-Brown was teaching at Chicago. Fred Eggan, the first American influenced by him, however, predicted that the Social Anthropology would eventually become more interested in diachronic studies; the researches by British anthropologists during the last two decades confirm such a synthesis. (Fred Eggan : 1954)

Another American anthropologist, Melferd Spiro, who carried on major field research in Micronesia and Burma, found Malinowski's approach quite rewarding. His work pertinently reveals Malinowski's approach explaining how culture serves individual needs. It also incorporates Radcliffe-Brown's views on function-serving interests of society. (Spiro : 1967 : 65-66)

Another American anthropologist, Goldschmidt (1974) proposed examining functional processes, as they are variously institutionalized in different societies with the object of determining whether similar processes for meeting special needs were present in all societies and if they were found not to be so uniformly present then accounting for their absence. Thus, Goldschmidt establishes the efficacy of functionalism not only for researches on particular societies but also for certain functional comparisons. A Canadian anthropologist, Cyril S. Belshaw (1970) also reflects Malinowski's impact on his work. Using concepts derived from Economics, he too wanted to know how successfully a particular culture meets its goal.

The functional-structural school, for obvious reasons, had a considerable influence on Indian Anthropology. Trained in the British tradition of anthropology, Indian anthropologists, like A. Aiyappan, D.N. Majumdar, M.N. Srinivas, K.S. Mathur, and T.N. Madan, carried on the tradition of Social Anthropology, particularly of functional-structural school to the fields of Indian studies. In their studies of the Nayar Polyandry etc. (A. Ayiappan : 1932, 1955), of the Ho tribe (D.N. Majumdar : 1950), the Coorg of Mysore (M.N. Srinivas : 1952), the Malwar village (K.S. Mathur : 1964), the Kashmiri Pandits (T.N. Madan : 1965), these scholars reflect the functional-structural tradition of British Social Anthropology and in their analyses reflect preferences for social integration, and functional dependence of the sub-systems in their limited unit of study. For methodological tools they are all for participant observation and vigorous field work traditions practised by their British teachers.

French Structuralism of Levi-Strauss

Linked up with the classical functional-structural school, certain recent theories with greater theoretical and methodological sophistication have been proposed and used. Among these theories, special mention may be made of French structuralism, led by Levi-Strauss. In a somewhat less comprehensive sense, structuralism refers to a mid-twentieth century movement in Linguistics, Folklore Research, Literary Criticism and Anthropology.

Roland Barthes (1972) terms Levi-Strauss's structuralism a movement whose object is, first to break down the subject, and then, to re-construct it in a way that shows the rules of functioning, the rules by which meaning is produced. Structural Anthropology has been used by Levi-Strauss (1963) primarily as a method for learning about the nature of thought and about the constraints imposed on thought by the human mind in producing it. He elaborates this approach in the study of myths : in analysing these he finds relationship of contrast and opposition—as, for example, between fire and water, sun and moon, raw and cooked food etc., which are pairs of mutually exclusive, yet complementary symbols. He extends his interpretations to discover the relationship between nature and culture and he finds all culture struggling with the distinction between itself and nature in mythical episodes, symbols and in the rules they establish. For example, the incest taboo is converting unregulated copulation present in nature into an orderly system of marriage as a characteristic of culture. By these devices, the opposition between nature and culture is transformed into different terms; the two realms are bridged and the tensions inherent between them are temporarily resolved (John J. Honnigmann : 1976 : 325). Levi-Strauss's structuralism is rather very comprehensive and covers varied fields in Anthropology, and, in a broad sense, takes into consideration the Marxist and the Freudian views in structuralism. Taken as a whole, he is the most prominent anthropologist whose worldwide popularity is almost unequalled in the contemporary time.

Ethnoscience

Following the concepts of formal semantic analysis, scholars like Sturtevent (1964), Anthony, F.C. Wallace, John Atkin (1960, 1965), Brent Berlin, Dennis E. Breadlove and Peter H. Raven (1968) have proposed a theory in Cultural Anthropology, variously known as 'ethno-science', 'ethno-linguistics', 'ethno-semantics'. It has been hailed as 'the new ethnography'. The techniques of Linguistics, used to improve the standards of ethnographic descriptions and analysis originated at Yale, spread rapidly through the United States. In this connection, the use of the terms ending in -'emic' (half of phonemics) and in -'etic' (half of phonetics), originally used by the missionary linguist, Kenneth Pike (1954: 8), were used to stress the 'structural result' obtained by phonemic analysis as opposed to the 'non-structural' results as characteristics of phonetics.

The use of these concepts and terms also became fashionable among a section of South Asian scholars, though they maintained their functional-structural model to interpret kinship and social system.

Systems of Symbols

In the systematic and integrative research of late, symbols have come to be identified with culture. The two important American anthropologists, David Schneider (1968) and Clifford Geertz (1973) conceived of culture as a system of meanings and of social relations as trafficking to symbols. It was rather a fresh approach to learn the cultural systems of a society in terms of symbols. This analysis, on the one hand, has been developed under the influence of Talcott Parson's concept of culture (Schnieder had studied under Talcott), and, on the other, with Levi-Strauss asserting that mental images-models have a reality of their own, and can be studied as perfectly objective facts.

Mary Douglas and Victor Turner carried out the study of

symbols. In her book, *National Symbols* (1970), Douglas stresses that symbols are the only means we have of communication. According to her, a symbol is the main instrument of thought and the only regulator of experiences. Victor Turner's contributions to the study of ritual symbolisation is most impressive. Turner, the British trained anthropologist who moved to Chicago in 1961, analyses ritual symbols in his ethnographic reports on the central African Ndembu. In the light of his ethnographic work, he terms ritual symbol as the smallest unit of ceremony. They consist of objects, activities, relationships, events, gestures, or spatial units, and their most important meaning refers to normative concepts generally held in a society. He also proposes the concept of dominant symbols. (Victor Turner : 1967)

Turner's theory of ritual symbolism has made considerable influence in the field of the study of religion and some young scholars have been using them in analysing their materials.

Interaction Theory

The study of the property of functional dependence was emphasized by Elliot D. Chapple and Carleton S. Coon as early as 1942 (Chapple and Coon : 1942) and was later followed in the book, *Culture and Behaviour*, published in 1970 (D. Chapple : 1970). The central theme of their theory is the concept of interaction between individuals, institutions, classes, etc. Equilibrium is another crucial concept and refers to the condition of a steady state maintained in individuals, institutions or a whole society. Such an approach to 'interaction' and 'equilibrium' evidently reminds one of Radcliffe-Brown approach though it finds new interpretations in the hands of the two American scholars. Walter Goldschmidt in an essay, proposes a methodology for the enquiry into the relation between the individual and society. He terms it as an ethnography of encounter by which he means the detailed recording of the interactions between two or more persons in the causes of significant events under natural conditions, and the full presentation of at least a selection of such records for public scrutiny. (Walter Goldschmidt : 1972 : 59-77)

While there is no denying the fact that the social interaction is the very stuff of human life and can be best studied under such methodological and theoretical leads, there are several value-loaded issues of Ethics involved in interfering with the society or individual under study. Such questions of ethics are also being raised in the contemporary anthropological enquiries.

Ecological Anthropology

The interaction between nature and man was long identified by Anthropo-geographers and ethnologists of historical and evolutionary schools. In case of human geographers, however, they emphasized geographical determinism. E.E. Evans Pritchard (1940) wrote about the Nuer, partly, in the same vein. It was realized in this quarter of the century that true relationship between culture and environment is one of the natural interactions. Redfield in his book *Little Community* (1955) reviews the studies to bring out the ecological basis of culture.

Laura Thompson took up a broad ecological approach, making the eco-cultural super-community her basic analytical unit—a human community viewed in both its biotic and social setting (L. Thompson : 1961). Within the super-community she saw the cultural eco-system conceived of as a system of goal-seeking devices operating to promote the community's biological survival.

Cultural Ecology directed its efforts at studying adaptation, features of geographical environment made by relatively isolated primitive societies. Such studies were also undertaken by Indian, Japanese and several other scholars in Africa. It was, however, questioned whether the ecological mode of explanation could be applied to complex societies.

Human Ethology

As a reaction to social determinism that had long obtained in social sciences, the human ethologists emphasized the need for understanding man in terms of his animal heritage. Robin Fox, a British anthropologist complained that cultural anthropology concentrating on cultural heritage acquired by human beings has taken too little an interest in what human beings brought with them across the bridge from nature to culture as part of their biological heritage (R. Fox : 1970). With this end in view, ethologists like Fox and his colleague Lionel Tiger (1971) made it their business to study the biological heritage for adaptation obtained by man from the period before any creature had attained human status.

Such a warning by the British ethologists is very well taken up by those social determinists who under the influence of British Social Anthropology have completely ignored the biological roots of culture. Anthropology as an integrative science in America and South Asia has, by and large, emphasized a bio-cultural approach. This movement of Human Ethology, however, is a timely reminder for counteracting the unbalanced approach that is fast developing among certain sections of anthropologists of the world, under the banner of a sociological or social science approach.

Psychological Anthropology

The development of Psychological Anthropology has been primarily an American endeavour, and is an evidence of the recognition of the need of inter-disciplinary approach among the disciplines of Anthropology, Sociology, Psychology and, to some extent, Biology. Such an inter-disciplinary approach before the 'fifties find reflected in the work of American anthropologists, like Mead (1928, 1930, 1935, 1937, 1949, 1951), Benedict (1934, 1946), Linton (1945) and G. Gorer (1948, 1949). Among the psychoanalysts mention may be made of Abraham Kardiner (1939, 1945) whose collaboration with anthropologists particularly Linton and Cora du Bois began around 1935.

While the inter-disciplinary approach in the study of culture and personality was established early, it found its systematization in the mid-'forties with the publication of Linton's book on *Cultural Background of Personality* in 1945 and also the organization of inter-disciplinary symposium on culture and personality in New York in November 1947 (S. Stanfeld Sargent and Mariam W. Smith : 1949). The symposium discussed the psychological and anthropological concepts and methods used in the inter-disciplinary frame and re-examined the major concepts of basic personality type and model personality structure in the broader frame. Similarly, Linton emphasized the need for the development of personality psychology jointly by anthropologists, sociologists and psychologists and, to some extent, biologists (R. Linton : 1945).

During the period under review, the theories and methods used in studying 'basic personality type' came for sharper scrutiny, further refinement and elaboration. Melford Spiro, with socialization studies in mind, protested against the one-sided attention paid to personality as the product of culture. As a confirmed functionalist, he urged to make culture and the social system the prime targets of research, with a view to learning how they are maintained through personality factor (M.E. Spiro : 1972). Publication of a volume on personality in nature, society, and culture emphasized the need of giving due attention to biological or individual factors in personality (C. Kluckhohn and Henry A. Murry : 1953). It was also pointed out that the ego-theorists like Erich Fromm had ignored biological needs as foundations of personality and emphasized more on the adaptation value of 'social character' (Erich Fromm : 1950, and Erich Fromm and Michael Maccoby : 1970).

The main impetus for the revolution in the methodology of culture and personality movement is derived from the work of W.M. Whiting and his collaborator Irvin Child. Under the collective influence of Cultural Anthropology, modern behavioral theory (specially of Clark K. Hall) and Neo-psychoanalysis, Whiting and Child present a cross-cultural study of child training and personality. In the light of their co-relational methods, with the sophisticated use of statistics, they confirm linkages between early childhood experience and adult customs. More convincingly than Kardiner or Fromm, their researches demonstrated how psychologically formative socialisation practices arise, and indicated that certain practices and resultant personality traits possess adaptive value in specific sociological context. They go on to corelate the linkage between childhood experiences and adult customs in the light of the different types of tribal societies found in different types of environment (John W.M. Whiting and Irvin L. Child : 1953).

The use of the statistical approach in search of co-relation and comparisons, as well as the use of the Human Relation Area Files, developed by Murdock and his associates, has been considered one of the major 'events in the social science of the past twenty years' (Campbell Donalt 1961 : 346). The statistical method used by Whiting and Child have certain limitations, no doubt, but it has been recognised by Marvin Harris (1968 : 453) as the only viable substitute for laboratory control.

Anthony F.C. Wallace makes a plea for developing psycho-biological approach to understand the ralationship between culture and personality. From the point of Cognitive Anthropology he feels the need for knowing about structures or processes in the brain whence from of organized knowledge arises. Referring to the work of psychoanalysts as well as structuralists like Levi-Strauss, he makes a plea for understanding the thought pattern and tendencies in the human mind (F.C. Wallace : 1972, 1973).

After a lapse of about two decades the Wenner-Gren Foundation hosted another conference on world views for which W.T. Jones wrote the basic paper (1972). In this paper, he refers to more than a dozen terms like 'world view' used by Redfield, 'ethos' by Bateson, 'style' by Kroeber, 'themes' by Opler, etc., and goes on to introduce a model in terms of which the various elements in a world view may be defined. After a lot of methodological exercise he defines world view concisely and precisely.

Jones goes on to give some examples of 'world view vectors', proposed model configuration, and applies them to the understanding of the world view of the 'Conference' itself. It is too early to judge the impact of his model for the study of world view. However, from the *Current Anthropology* treatment, it is clear that it has not been able to cut much ice, though there seems to be a general agreement about its precision in definition and its possible utility in field work.

In spite of its inter-disciplinary popularity in America, Psychological Anthropology was ignored by British social anthropologists and others who were under the influence of functional-structural school. Their institution-based analysis of society could not be moulded to accept the individual as the unit of study. Some of them, like Julian Pitt Rivers, however, felt the need of using the concept 'social character' instead of accepting individual-based concept of basic personality type.

The Soviet Ethnography also found it unpalatable to give importance to individual in the analysis of society and culture. The psychological techniques, again, have not found acceptance as a tool of analysis. In recent years, however, the concept of 'ethno-psychology' is being mentioned in some researches and a few researches from psychological angle have been conducted on the ethnic communities by the scientists of the Institute of Ethnography at Moscow.

In the European countries, in general, the dominance of ethnological research is so great that theoretical and methodological premises of Psychological Anthropology so far find no place.

In India, under the general influence of American Anthropology, a section on Psychological Anthropology was established in Anthropological Survey of India during the 'fifties and research on the intelligence of the tribals was initiated. Since then, the use of the psychological angle and the application of psychological techniques including Rorschach and T.A.T. for continued field work among the tribes has highlighted the personality characteristics of several tribal groups.

3 | European Anthropology

EUROPE has been a meeting place of varied anthropological traditions. If the western Europe, especially Great Britain and France, have mainly practised Anthropology as the science of 'others' culture' (land and people of their colonies), the central European countries, especially Hungary, Poland, Yugoslavia, Germany, etc., have confined the science to the study of their own ethnic and tribal groups. Again, the western social anthropologists studied the natives of the other countries primarily under the influence of functional-structural school, laying the least emphasis on history. The central European ethnology, on the other hand, incorporating within itself archaeological, folkloric and humanistic traditions, has been strongly oriented towards ethno-history. This unique ethnological and ethno-historical tradition has been recently named as Regional Ethnography or National Ethnography. (Hultkrantz : 1960 : 202-203)

The ethnological tradition of central Europe, the status of which was reported by the Yugoslavian anthropologist, Ivanicek, to the International symposium at New York, has remained more or less unaltered (1953 : 347-48). Physical Anthropology (which continues to be known as Anthropology, the science of man) has maintained its independent identity and has continued to thrive since 1876 when the VIII International Congress of Anthropology was organized at Budapest. In 1876, again,

Physical Anthropology (Anthropology) became a subject of syllabus in public schools in Hungary. Four years later, the first chair of anthropology was established at the Pazmany University in Budapest (Maday Bela C. : 1968 : 181). In Yugoslavia, however, before the Second World War, there was not a single institution associated with (Physical) Anthropology, Ethnology, Ethnography, Sociology, Linguistics, Pre-History, Archaeology, etc. which are still considered distinct disciplines and have other traditions. A survey of this field by Thomas Hofer (1968 : 311-315) brings out differences in approach, method and knowledge within each of these areas. Even the terms in national language (Volkskunde Folk-livesforskning, neprajz, narodopis, etc.) are not congruous in meaning. In view of these and uprooted distinctiveness the anthropological developments made in the United States has gone virtually unnoticed in the central European countries. While reviewing Hungarian Anthropology, the reasons for this poor state of communication has been summarised by Maday, as : (*1*) language difficulty, (*2*) divergent disciplinary interests, (*3*) differences in classification of various sub-disciplines and their practitioners between Europe and United States, and (*4*) international political tensions. (Maday : 1968 : 180)

With increasing contacts, the American anthropologists are surprised by the fragmentation of the specific fields of Anthropology in European universities, museums and institutions. For instance, Physical Anthropology is in the medical school, the folk components of national culture is part of humanities, and does not include the study of folk culture out of Europe. Similarly, Europeans are astonished to see that Americans are capable of grasping the enormous range of Anthropology, and often doubt whether human intellect is capable of such a performance at all. (Hultkrantz : 1965)

In spite of their paradoxes and surprises, it has been realized by several central European ethnographers that the adaptation of a number of anthropological concepts and theories might benefit national ethnographers. On the other hand, it has also been declared openly that a wholesale adaptation of American Anthropology would be a step backwards (Hultkrantz : 1965 : 18). Hofer (1968 : 315) raises a note of caution against the *missionary zeal* of the American to *convert* the central European ethnologists to community studies of the American brand. He observes :

> American anthropology is a vigorous expanding discipline which continually conquer new territories. The national ethnography of central Europe also appears to be thriving if not at the same rate as north American anthropology.

Hofer, in another context, remarks that both anthropologists and ethnographers have their own task in the exploration of Europe. However, he deplores the over-emphasis by American and other foreign anthropologists on the study of the oppressive past, peasant morals of vanishing villages, and backward societies and communities. He makes a plea that it would be more scientific to insert into this picture the colourful, rich, intricate fabric of culture processes which the ethnographers have explored and described in a language differing from those of the anthropologists. (Hofer : 1968 : 315)

Anthropology in USSR

A reference may also be made about the status of Anthropology in the USSR. In terms of communication, contacts and disciplinary classification, USSR shares similar problems as central Europe. The term Anthropology for them means the same as Physical Anthropology, while the term Ethnology approximates to the use of the term Cultural Anthropology though the studies are confined only to the backward and folk communities of Soviet Union and elsewhere. The study of the urban and advanced rural communities fall under a separate discipline of Sociology. The physical anthropological researches and teachings have old traditions and are confined to a few universities. The ethnological research finds place in the ethnographic and historical institutes located in important capitals of the National Republics. In addition to Moscow, Leningrad, Tashkent, Kieve even the smaller units like Tbilisi and Sukhumi in the South are doing valuable work in the respective regions. The Institutes of Ethnography, however, located in Moscow and Leningrad, house most of the Soviet ethnographers who specialize on the ethnic groups, and areas of the different parts of the world.

The anthropological researches in the Soviet Union have also got exposed to wider contact since their participation in the International Congress of Anthropological and Ethnological Sciences in 1956. The contacts got accelerated when the VIIth World Congress (ICAES) was held in Moscow. During this Congress the Soviet scholars were exposed to the manifold developments made by Anglo-Saxon scholars. Anthropologists of the rest of the world also got a first hand knowledge about Soviet Ethnography, their rich museums and specialized centres of post-graduate teaching and research.

With the additional stimulation generated by the World Congress, Soviet Ethnography has evidently enriched itself and expanded its coverage to the extent the political ideology could permit. Several Soviet scholars went to Socialist or other friendly countries of the world for brief spells of field work. The two ethnographic centres of Moscow and Leningrad also received ethnologists from other Socialist countries as well as their own institutions for prolonged and advanced training. The exchange of ethnographers with some of the other friendly countries is also being promoted. Under such programmes, Soviet ethnographers like M.K. Kudriatsev and N.N. Cheboksarov made repeated visits to India. As a result of their field researches in collaboration with other colleagues specialising on South Asia, they have published a work of several volumes on the peoples of Asia. While most of their writings are in Russian, a few papers in English—on Asia (S.I. Brunk, N.N. Cheboksarov and Y.V. Chesnow : 1975 : 182-211 and Cheboksarov 1964), Modern Africa (R.N. Ismagclova : 1974), Oceania (P.I. Puckkov : 1974), Eastern Asia (V.A. Robin : 1964)—have also been published by Soviet ethnographers.

Under the exchange programme, I had occasion to visit the important anthropological centres of Soviet Union for a couple of months in 1974. The development in ethnographic studies between 1964 (when I visited the country for the first time) and then in 1974 was quite impressive. The ethnographic institutes had recruited more staff and expanded their foreign area research programmes. The smaller institutes, which were in infancy in 1964, also had by then strengthened and developed new ethnographic programmes. The Institute of Tbilisi in Georgia, for example, prepared an ethnographic atlas of Georgia and established an open air museum on the traditional life and culture of the Georgian, under the guidance of a Georgian ethnographer, Academician Chitaya. The researches of lady ethnographers, S.A. Maretina and Volchock, on north-eastern India were further intensified, though the latter shifted from the ethnographic study to the archaeological study of India. The historical study of M.G. Levin (1972) brought adequate evidence to establish that the ancient Indians were both linguistically and culturally closer to the Iranians. Several scholars including Y.V. Arutunyan published papers on Korea, and Y.V. Maretin published on Indonesia (1964). Most of these papers were based on the literary sources as the Soviet ethnographers field researches continued to be very restricted. I came across several scholars who had published ethnographic material on the nomads and had helped in their sedentarization programmes.

The basic theoretical orientation of the ethnological researches in Soviet Union is neo-evolutionism, reference to which has been made earlier. A new theory in Soviet Union has been proposed by Y.V. Broomley (1974 : 17-44). Broomley refers to 'synthetic formation' of homogeneo-heterogeneous ethnic formations, which he defines as ethno-social organism. Ethnos in more general term is the combination of racial, linguistic, historical interactions within and between the communities and typology of the various nations may be presented in it. In the absence of its application, however, the theory of ethnos continues to be vague to us and even to some of the Soviet ethnographers.

Anthropology in the Two Germanies

Similar traditions of museum and library researches continue in the German Democratic Republic (GDR). In course of my visit to Berlin, Dresdon Leipzig and Rostok I came across publications on ethno-history of the selected tribes on which the different scholars specialized. The Ideological studies based on Sanskrit texts is particularly strong at Halle which functioned as an old centre of Sanskrit learning. At Dresden a couple of scholars including Lydia Teke Schwalbe had published some papers based on the museum materials on the Oraons of Central

India. At Leipzig, again, using the museum materials, a book and a few papers were published on the Nagas of north-eastern India. At Berlin, I came across several ethnologists including Frank Reiter who were comparing museum materials of selected countries or tribes.

The GDR, so far, had not participated in the International Congress of Anthropological and Ethnological Sciences. In 1975, for the first time, it accepted our invitation to be the member of the Permanent Council and sent its delegation under the leadership of Prof. Shelnou to ICAES held in Rome. It is expected that with the increasing contacts the speed of development of German Ethnology will be accelerated. As the situation stands, the American influence in these Socialist countries is conspicuously absent.

Like other central European countries, West Germany, Italy and Greece have older traditions of physical anthropological research. In the name of ethnological researches, the West German scholars have been considerably influenced by the current American traditions. With direct contacts with several American professors including L. Krader in the University of Berlin, the American influence, in contrast with that in East Germany, has percolated considerably. It specially finds reflected in the organization of Interdisciplinary Institute on South Asia at Heidelberg, where ethnologists are working on rural and urban problems of India, in coordination with specialists of 13 related disciplines. The American influence is also reflected in the structure and function of the German Research Council, which is the chief funding organization for researches in West Germany.

The Italian Anthropological Tradition

In the field of Ethnology, though Italian travellers visited far off countries and brought home peculiar items of material culture even in the sixteenth century, Ethnology remained rather a late-comer to Italy. It was in 1958 that the Institute of Ethnology for a post-graduate training and research was established there. The ethnological researches under the guidance of Prof. Grottanelli of Rome University has made tremendous progress during the last 20 years, and there are now 11 professors in

Ethnology at various institutions in the different parts of Italy.

The Italian ethnologists have also focussed their attention on the study of the cultural history which is the main trend of Italian Ethnology. Next to cultural history their interests are on the backward communities of Italy and certain primitive tribes in far off lands. Among them, mention may be made of L. Cipriani who stayed among the negrito tribe of Adaman; his pioneering work on them was published as a posthumous book (Lidio Cipriani : 1969).

Taken on the whole, the European Ethnology was once a source of considerable inspiration and its influences, in general, radiated even upto Japan before the world wars. With the increasing American influence, however, both the west European Social Anthropology and central European Ethnology were overwhelmed by the American cultural anthropological traditions. To some extent the European tradition of historical Ethnology and self study has been retained. A large section of European anthropologists have responded favourably to emerge out of the American tradition.

4 Anthropology in South Asia

India

THE rise of Anthropology in India and its current trends are very well covered in several papers published from time to time (S.C. Roy : 1922, D.N. Majumdar : 1950A, 1956, G.S. Ghurey : 1956, S.C. Dube : 1962, N.K. Bose : 1963, L.P. Vidyarthi : 1966A, 1966B, Surajit Sinha : 1968). During this decade R.K. Jain (1971), Surajit Sinha (1971), Gopal Sarana and Dharni P. Sinha (1976), M.S. Gore (N.D.) have made critical appraisal of the foreign influences on Indian Anthropology. Under the auspices of the ICSSR, the development in different fields of Anthropology and Sociology were reviewed by competent specialists in three volumes (ICSSR : 1972, 1974). In a two-volume publication, the present author has surveyed the rise of Indian Social/Cultural Anthropology covering the fields of tribal, rural, urban, caste, folklore and psychological studies. (L.P. Vidyarthi : 1977)

There is a general agreement that the formative period of Indian Anthropology (1774-1919) dominated by the British administrators was followed by the constructive period (1920-1947) when both Indian and British anthropologists, like Rivers, Marrett Frazer and Malinowski jointly worked in this field. After India's Independence, as the contacts with the American-scholars increased, Indian Anthropology entered its analytical period and made manifold developments, reference to which will follow in some detail.

Anthropology in India owes its birth to the British colonial policy, and takes us back to 1774 when the Asiatic Society of Bengal was established at Calcutta to take up researches on 'nature and man'. Since then British administrators, foreign missionaries, British judges, travellers and army men continued to publish material on the tribes and castes primarily with a view to ensuring smooth colonial administration by acquainting the administrators about the natives' habitat, social institutions, religious beliefs, economic condition, etc. Such an objective finds on official confirmation when Risley observes that they were undertaken by British administration "to enable the rulers to take stock of their position and to see how it has faired with the people committed to their change." (Risley : 1903)

While the researches in South Asia continued with this expressed policy by the British administrators, the British anthropologists like Rivers (1906), Seligmann (1911), Radcliffe-Brown (1922) and Hutton (1931), who worked on the tribes of South Asia, were the late comers.

Till the 'fifties, it was the primary occupation of the British and Indian anthropologists to study the tribes. The economists with one exception of Wiser (1936) studied the villages, and the sociologists concentrated on the study of cities. Majumdar refers to this monopoly even in 1956. (D.N. Majumdar : 1956 : 171-73)

Village Studies

A break from this traditional pre-occupation occurred towards the middle of the century when anthropologists began village studies in a big way as well as included urban studies within the purview of their research.

This change over from tribal studies to village studies can be mainly explained in terms of greater contact on the personal as well as institutional levels between Indian and American cultural anthropologists interested in village studies; and secondly, the needed widespread concern with rural development in India. Initially, American anthropologists, like Morris Opler of Cornell University, Oscar Lewis of the University of Illinois, David Mandelbaum of the University of California-Berkeley,

McKim Marriott of University of Chicago, and several of their students came and stayed in India and created an atmosphere (*a*) for the systematic study of Indian villages with a view to testing certain hypotheses, (*b*) for refining some of the methodological framework developed elsewhere, and (*c*) to assess the community development programmes in villages.

Along with these American anthropologists, in the 'fifties, Dube (1955), Srinivas (1955), Majumdar (1950) and a few other Indian anthropologists were stimulated to take up analytical study of rural communities in India, and in the real sense of the term Indian anthropological researches which, so far, were limited to British colonial pattern became integrated with the world literature on Anthropology.

Complex Societies

Among the researches of American scholars, special mention may be made of Robert Redfield, Milton Singer, McKim Marriott of Chicago University whose work in theory and methodology leads to understanding the folk, peasant and urban communities as dimensions of Indian civilization. The concepts of 'great' and 'little' traditions, proposed and used by them, provided a new and effective perspective to understand Indian civilization. It led to the beginning of an anthropological approach to the study of civilization in terms of the complex structure of 'great' and 'little' traditions. The Chicago school further stimulated Indian scholars to study the traditional and modern cities in terms of their orthogeneity or heterogeneity or folk-urban continuum, etc. At the urban development and planning level, again, the National Planning Commission sponsored and financed a number of large-scale studies of urban and industrial complexes, including a few in the tribal belts, in which anthropologists played key roles.

A quantitative analysis of such sociological and anthropological researches of community studies has been recently made by Chekki (1974) which brings out certain interesting facts regarding the theoretical and methodological basis of the community studies in India during 1947-1972. A bibliographical survey of 5,226 published and unpublished studies reveals that rural and urban community studies in India have been predominantly empirical specially using primary data. In most cases they used techniques of interview, questionnaire and observation while a vast portion of community research was of microscopic nature. Comparative, cross national, longitudinal and/or quasi-experimental studies are conspicuous by their absence.

Further testing of hypotheses and building of theories has not been a major concern of any researcher. It thus confirms the general notion that village and urban studies in India have been more influenced by the American social anthropologists than the sociologists who are more quantitative and model-building researchers. The questionnaire technique, however, has become widespread in social anthropological studies and in the name of quasi-quantification of data the questionnaires are applied even in the study of the pre-literate tribal communities as interview scheduled.

Psychological Studies

Under the same American influence the study of culture and personality found a place in the Anthropological Survey of India during the early 'fifties under the guidance of B.S. Guha, a graduate from Harvard University. Several psychologists, specially Uma Chaudhury and P.C. Ray of the Survey, undertook field researches specially among the tribals with a view to establishing differences, personality types and other socio-psychological characteristics. The socio-psychological researches received further impetus when American anthropologist, Geehal P. Steed, conducted field researches in a Hindu village in Gujarat, and G.M. Carstairs, a British psychiatrist, studied the personality formation among different communities of Rajasthan. The psycho-cultural researches are being conducted with increased impetus and financial assistance in the Survey and in the departments of Anthropology and Sociology in several universities including Allahabad, Ranchi and Utkal. A full-length survey of Psychological Anthropology in India has been made by this author elsewhere. (Vidyarthi : 1969A)

Power Structure and Leadership

The attempt to analyse power structure and decision-making processes also came in prominence with the village studies. The initial stimulation to undertake these studies goes to an American professor, Oscar Lewis and his Indian collaborator H.S. Dhillon who did field researches and published two volumes on faction and leadership in north and south Indian villages respectively (Oscar Lewis : 1954, and H.S. Dhillon : 1955). These much-talked of two volumes, published under the auspices of Planning Commission, brought to light the varied roles of kin-and-caste-oriented factions in the decision-making process in rural India. These studies further inspired a number of other American, British and Indian scholars to take up other kinds of study of rural leadership in India.

Applied and Action Research

The tribal and rural community development programme of Government of India gave further fillip to anthropologists to study and evaluate the processes of change in tribal and rural India. The approaches of Applied Anthropology developed during the colonial rule persisted. The concept of Action Anthropology formulated by Sol Tax in America partly replaced the principles of Applied Anthropology. In some of the later writings of Indian scholars, like Majumdar (1949), Dube (1960), Elwin (1958), Vidyarthi (1957, 1968) and a few others, the influence of Action Anthropology emphasizing the concepts of self-determination and volition of values find prominently reflected.

With manifold developments in anthropological researches, challenge has been posed to Indian anthropologists to act as social doctors to help the administration at the various levels of diagnosing social ills, in prescribing appropriate remedies, and smoothening the course of transformation from traditional to transitional, and then perhaps to 're-organisational' phase of our society. In the democratic set up of our country this realisation has marked the beginning of a new phase in planning and implementation, where hopefully, administrators and social scientists are attempting to work together to induce social and economic development among the tribal, rural and urban population of India. The pattern of such collaborations may be briefly enumerated in terms of five categories.

The first category of the Applied Anthropologists is of those who act as consultant on the staff of the administration, and usually function under the control of the administrator. Under this category falls a large number of anthropologists working in various stations of Anthropological Survey of India, numerous State-managed tribal research institutes and numerous cells and departments of the Central and State Governments in India.

The second type is of such outsider anthropologist consultants to the administrator as are not on the regular pay roll of the organization. Among them are numerous university professors who work on the government-sponsored committees and advise the administration on tribal and other social issues.

The third type constitutes the category in which the researcher and administrator work together as co-administrators. While there are numerous anthropologists of the earlier two types there are very few of this and the next two categories.

The fourth category is represented by just one anthropologist who is in actual charge of the development programme of a tribe (the Lodha) which he and his associates have been developing and studying for the last 25 years. (P.K. Bhowmick : 1963)

The last category is represented by Action Anthropology of Sol Tax which can function only in an independent manner, and in institutions where an action anthropologist can combine both action and research (Sol Tax : 1959). Though the term action research has become well known in India, its implications differ in different situations as the ideal situation free from outside intervention in action programme is rarely available. Efforts have recently been made, however, by Ranchi University to apply some of these concepts in the study of the Birhor. The constraints, and interventions, are so great that the efforts are likely to be abandoned.

Thus, on account of an overall realisation of the importance of cultural, enthnic, religious, political and other non-economic factors in the development strategy, the corresponding role of the social anthropologists have found recognition in a big way during the period under review. Such a realisation in case of social anthropologists is being reflected in their involvement with the central and state governments and with the series of tribal research institutes, the census operations, the National Council of Educational Training and Research, family planning organisations, Space Research Centre, and several other such organisations interested in developmental and modernization programmes. In addition, social anthropologists are getting associated with urban planning, labour research, youth research, political movements and studies of military organisations. A survey of such publications is found at several places, special reference, however, may be made to T.B. Naik (1972) and Vidyarthi (1968, 1976B, 1977).

The vast literature that has been published on the various areas related to innovation, development, modernisation, etc., deserve to be meaningfully examined so that they may lead to the development of theories in the sub-discipline of Applied and Action Anthropology. During this quarter of century, which covers the entire period of our implementation of five Five-year Plans in India, manifold efforts for modernizing a tradition- bound civilization have been made. Owing to this varied, multi-dimensional, multi-national experience, India is able to furnish rich material and view points to formulate certain generalisations and theories in the field of Applied and Action Anthropology.

Study of Religion

The study of religion as practised by the people at different levels of development has been a fascinating theme for research by social anthropologists. An analytical study of primitive religion in India was initiated by Majumdar (1942, 1950B) and his explanation of Bongaism in its final form, in the affairs of a tribe falls in line with the modern anthropological trends in the study of religion. A full-length study of tribal religion, however, was published by Elwin on the Savera tribe of Orissa (1955) in which he supports the concept of 'spiritism' in relation to the concept of 'Mana'. The study of religion in the context of Indian villages was initiated by Srinivas (1952) who developed the concept of Sanskritization to explain the process of change in a Hindu village. These studies reflect the influence of functional-structural approach viewed in tribal and rural context in India.

The focus of interest of cultural anthropologists in the study of religion during the 'sixties is embodied in the preparation of two volumes—one edited by me (1961) and the other by E.B. Harper (1964). Both these volumes include papers by mainly *Indian and American* cultural anthropologists, on different aspects of tribal and rural religions based upon their original investigation.

Among recent publications, mention may be made of studies on Sacred Complex (Vidyarthi : 1961; M. Jha : 1971; B.N. Saraswati : 1976; Vidyarthi and Jha : 1974) which endeavours to understand Indian civilization in relation to sacred complexes of the ancient places of pilgrimage. The several publications of Chicago anthropologists Milton Singer, B.S. Cohn, McKim Marriott have endeavoured to interpret Indian tradition in the light of textual and contextual meterials. Their contributions embodied in a special volume edited by Singer and Cohn (1968) have given theoretical and methodological leads to understand Indian civilization in all its complexities.

Folklore Researches

Though India provides a rich laboratory for the study of folklore, its recognition as an independent discipline is yet to be established. From the surveys of the Indian folkloric researches done by Durga Bhagvat (1958), Shankar Sengupta (1964), Indradeva and Vidyarthi (1972), one comes to know how folklore, which was recognised as part of Indology, is getting oriented to the social science approach. Initially, the approach to folklore researches was confined to collections of songs and tales. Only recently with the researches of Verrier Elwin (1944, 1954), K.D. Upadhyay (1957), P.D. Goswami (1960), Dulal Choudhary (1973) and several others, the folklore researches have entered the stage of their classifications and partial interpretations. These interpretations, however, remained one of Boasian type interpreting them as 'tribal epic'.

Some of the scholars trained abroad, however, are applying the Thomson's index and Levi-Strauss's structural approach for the analysis of the folktales and myths. In the analysis of the folktales of Assam, Goswami (1960), finds Thomson's methods quite rewarding. Jawaharlal Handoo (1976) makes a case for the application of Levi-Strauss's structural approach to the analysis of the folklore. In a recent All-India Congress of Folklore the implications of the 'motif' and 'structural approach' were discussed in the light of concrete researches. In adopting the sophisticated tools of analysis, thus, the influence of the French and the American approaches have very much pronounced its own disciplinary configuration. The folklore studies are heading towards carving out of its own disciplinary configuration. Along with that, due emphasis is laid on quality. The institutional support is also likely to play an increased role. Recently the University of Mysore has started a full-fledged Department of Folklore under a Professor. The Central Institute of Indian Languages as well as the Anthropological Survey of India too have plans to strengthen their folklore units. The number of departments of Anthropology, Linguistics and Literature, offering folklore as a special group or a paper within the respective disciplines is increasing.

Tribal Ethnography

The initial British tradition of studying tribes and castes by colonial administration for colonial purposes, supplemented by the British anthropologists like, Rivers, Seligmann, Radcliffe-Brown found a big jump with the entry of Verrier Elwin (1939, 1943A, 1943B, 1947) and C. von Furer-Haimendorf (1943, 1945A, 1945B). Both before and after India's independence, these two scholars—Elwin and Furer-Haimendorf—continued to write monographs on the tribes, and tribal problems in India. Elwin under the influence of functional school wrote his celebrated book on *The Muria and the Ghotul* (1947), *The Religion of An Indian Tribe* (1955) and then wrote his book on *A Philosophy for NEFA* (1958). During post-independence era, Furer-Haimendorf revisited some of the Himalayan areas and published his monograph on the Naga (1953) and the NEFA tribes (1962). In the recent times he has re-inforced his proposal of re-study, and is currently engaged in the study of Gonds in Andhra Pradesh which he studied about three decades ago.

Taken on the whole, except the sporadic efforts of Majumdar (1962), Elwin (1958) and Vidyarthi (1963), systematic and scientific tribal studies sustained a set-back till the mid-'sixties. Even the census operation of India, which has long and rich tradition of including tribal studies, gave relatively more importance to village studies, fairs and festivals and material culture in the 1961 census, and ignored tribal ethnography.

After the mid-'sixties the Indian Institute of Advanced Study organised an international symposium in Simla on Urgent Anthropology in India (B.L. Abbi and S. Saberwal: 1969) which reiterated the need to study the tribes on urgent basis. This urgency was re-inforced when the Institute organized another All-India Seminar on Tribal Situation in India (K.S. Singh : 1972). In Ranchi also a series of nine seminars was held to highlight the varied problems of development (1968), urbanization (1969) and industrialization (1970), leadership (1966) and social movements, and tensions in the tribal areas of India (1969). A few scholars, such as F.G. Bailey (1958, 1960) from Great Britain, and Burling (1963) and Edward Jay (1970) from America further gave fillip to tribal studies with the use of their sophisticated methodology and interpretation of facts under refined theories.

B.K. Roy Burman as the officer in-charge of the social studies in Census has, during the last two decades, published profusely on the tribals, particularly of the North-Eastern region. In a recent paper on a second look at tribal ethnography in India (1977) he draws our close attention to the negative aspects of tribal ethnographic studies. He examines them broadly under the three categories of idealogical, methodological and substantive type of limitations. He complains of the absence of historical vision, arrogance of great traditions, lack of comparative method, poor instruments of analysis as the limiting factors of our ethnographic research. He also refers to the colonial hang-over in our tribal research and tribal policies which distort our perspective.

Two of the recent publications, the *Tribal Culture of India* by this author (Vidyarthi and Rai :1977) and *Tribal Heritage of India* (*Ed.* S.C. Dube : 1977) endeavour to provide a comparative summary of the findings of scholars on various Indian tribes. Such efforts need to be further intensified with a view to getting an integrated picture of tribal life and culture in the national perspective.

Kinship and Family Study in India

In addition to tribal ethnography, the carry over of the rich British tradition is found in the study of kinship in India. The first scientific and most outstanding study by any professional anthropologist in India dates back to 1906 when W.H.R. Rivers published his book on Social Organization of the Polyandrous Toda (W.H.R. Rivers : 1906). The rich tradition in kinship study, initiated by him on the basis of his direct field work and application of genealogical method was followed up by his students, K.P. Chattopadhyay and G.S. Ghurey. They carried on the kinship study, along with other themes, in their respective departments of Anthropology at Calcutta and Sociology at Bombay. Under their guidance this field of study became quite popular. A series of researches were undertaken in India by Indian and foreign scholars which have recently been reviewed by Leela Dube (L. Dube : 1974 : 233-366). Her brilliant survey shows how over these past few decades varied criteria and principles, such as those developed by Kirchoff and Lowie (R.H. Lowie : 1950), A.L. Kroeber (1909), G.P. Murdock (1949) and A.E. Radcliffe-Brown (1941, 1950, 1952), have been used in the analysis of kinship terms in India.

Of late, in the study of Indian kinship, L. Dumout (1953, 1957) occupies a special place. His theoretical formulation springs from the application of Levy-Strauss's structural principle of complementary dualism on logical principle of opposition, which is regarded as a fundamental feature of the human mind. The Japanese scholars, Chie Nekane (1968) during her field study of the Garo and Khasi make an analytical description of the Khasi social organization and Khasi kinship structure. Her typology brings the Garo on the comparative map of the matrilineal system of the world. R. Burling (1963) also studied the Garo tribe and provided excellent data on the various features of kinship, marriage and family such as on matrilocal, own cousin marriage and households, kinship groupings, mother-in-law marriage and so on.

Among several other foreign scholars, mention may be made of K. Gough (1952,a,b,c) who offers cogent description of the matrilineal units of the Nayar kinship, and of Joan Mencher

(1962) who discusses the changes in role relationship among closely related matrilineal kin, between spouses, and with the spouse's kin. Among the village studies dealing with kinship extensively and intensively, in its various aspects, mention may be made of Adrian C. Mayer's *Caste and Kinship in Central India* (1960). Mayer's endeavour to understand the native categories in the field of kinship is significant. The more provocative generalizations regarding the structure and content of Hindu kinship system and its effects on Hindu personality and social system come from Francis L.K. Hsu (1963). The contrast drawn between the Chinese and the Indian way of life is particularly striking. In the Chinese family, the central relationship is between father and son, while among the Hindus the mother-son tie is the most important.

Among the Indian scholars, special mention may be made of Irawati Karve, T.N. Madan, R.K. Mukherjee, B. Mukherjee, etc. Karve, who is noted for her pioneering work on Indian kinship, made a comparative study of kinship of four cultural zones—the Northern, the Central, the Southern and the Eastern (Irawati Karve : 1953). In addition to extended field work, her use of ancient tests is of considerable importance; it presents an analytical description of the family system of the Pandits of rural Kashmir in the wider context of their kinship organization. This is, by far, the only full-length published study focusing entirely on family and kinship as they function within Hindu Society. Originally written as a doctoral thesis, under the guidance of S.F. Nadel at Australian National University in Canbera, it reflects the impact of British Social Anthropology.

Along with kinship, the study of Indian family primarily in terms of jointness and nuclearity has been a central theme. Mukherjee's recent book, *Family in India : A Perspective* (1969) presents a novel and fruitful approach for the understanding of family-structure in India. Instead of making naive assumption regarding the change in family organization, he uses an analytical inductive approach to make a concrete application of demographic data to answer the questions like : *Are Joint Family structures in India being nuclearized in course of time* ?

In spite of the rich tradition of kinship and family studies in India, Dube complains about the declining state of this sub-field in Social Anthropology. At one place, she observes : "Among

Indian social anthropologists and sociologists, in general, and among the new generation of students of these disciplines in particular, kinship has lost some ground." (1974 : 327)

As regards the cause of decline, she refers to the growing feeling that in the contemporary context, kinship as an organizing principle is no longer as important as it used to be in the past. Secondly, she notes that anthropologists like to keep away from the study of kinship as it is linked with primordial loyalties in the political and economic spheres and their manipulation for personal gains. In addition, I guess, the study of kinship reminds one of theoretical involvement of colonial brand British Anthropology, which has become unfashionable in the progressive and advanced countries like the United States.

Anthropological Organizations in India

At the organizational level, there are 16 departments of Anthropology, which offer Master's degree in the subject, while there are two which offer Master's degree in Human Biology (Andhra and Patiala). Recently, four Departments of Social Anthropology along with Sociology have been established at Shillong, Patiala, Silliguri and Behrampur. There are 12 tribal research institutes located in the States with tribal concentration, which specialize in applied anthropological researches. In addition, at the national level, Anthropological Survey of India was established in 1946, with its headquarters at Calcutta having six regional centres. This organization carries on anthropological research of both fundamental and applied nature.

These departments, institutes and the national survey organization have broadened the perspective of Anthropology, and except a very few centres, they practise integrated and wholistic approach in Anthropology. In the body constituted as the Indian Council of Social Science Research (1968), Anthropology is represented, though for the purposes of grants, of the projects supported by this body, ones with social science content get preference. This trend to exclude or minimise the biological aspect of man in Anthropology and equate Social Anthropology with Sociology has found resistance from the professional organisations of anthropologists. The trend has been generated partly because of the 'defection' of some anthropologists to the sociological institutions and departments, and partly because of inter-disciplinary inter-actions among basic social sciences, particularly Social Anthropology and Sociology.

Pakistan

Though the neighbouring country of Pakistan has given the least attention to the development of anthropological studies in its universities and institutes, applied research concerned with the social, economic and demographic problems of the country has received considerable attention. This over-involvement in pragmatic researches has resulted both in and against of both fundamental research and theory. The Post-Graduate Institute of Social Sciences at the University of Islamabad, social science research centres at the universities of Punjab, and Lahore, the Charter for Pakistan Academy for Rural Development at Peshawar, confirm the same orientation.

Ravindra Jain (1971) in a review of anthropological development in Pakistan points out :

> In Pakistan, a new nation rather than a renewed one like India, the concern with developing social and human Sciences is on a more restricted and manageable scale. It is, to that extent, also more amenable to careful social engineering. Philosophical issues, like those of India, do not in Pakistan skew the ideology of historical development and change.

Among the important publications of foreign scholars which have led to the theoretical contributions of significant nature, mention may be made of Norwegian Scholar Barth's work on *Principles of Social Stratification* (1953, 1960) and American scholar Robert Pehrson's book on a similar theme of social organization of the Baluchi (1966). Barth's study of Swat in North Pakistan identifies the social groups with seven-fold hierarchical order : (*1*) persons of holy descent, (*2*) land-owners and administrators, (*3*) preists, (*4*) craftsmen, (*5*) agricultural tenants and labourers, (*6*) herders, and (*7*) despised group (1960 : 127). Both Barth and Pehrson bring out the certain elements of inherent instability in integration. Their overall approach and interpretation of the data are on functional-structural frame. The people of Pakistan, have been viewed in the historical context by U.V. Gankovsky of Moscow (1971).

Among the native scholars, who are very few in number and almost none in Anthropology, mention may be made of M.S. Choudhary and M.A. Khan (1964) who made sociological analysis of Pakistan Society and of S.M. Ikram (1955) who made a social historical appraisal of Pakistan heritage with Western historian, Percival Spear. An Indian, U.T. Thakur (1959) studied the Sindhi culture, based on the literary sources.

Bangladesh

Bangladesh is still the most unresearched country. Anthropology as an academic discipline has not received recognition in the Bangladeshi universities. Some field researches have been conducted by American scholars among the hill tribes of Chittagong (D.E. Sopher: 1963, 1964) and among the Bengali villagers (Mary Jone Beech, Peter J. Bertocei and Laman A. Corwin: 1966). While studying the Chakma tribe, Sopher dealt with population dislocation (1963) and Swidden researched on wet-rice cultivation (1964) in the Chittagong hills. In their six papers in the edited volume, Mary Jone Beech and others, working under the influence of American tradition of village studies, bring out rich ethnographic materials about Bangla villages.

Among native social scientists, mention may be made of A.K. Nazmul Karim (1956) who made a comparative study of social change and social stratification in India and Pakistan (Bangladesh). S.M. Hafeez Zaidi (1970) under the American influence studied the changing village culture of the Bangladesh.

Ceylon

As a part of the same British colonial tradition as in India, the tribes and people of Ceylon, were studied for long by the British Administration. The Vedda tribe was studied by the British anthropologist, G.G. Seligmann and B.G. Seligmann as early as 1911. During the period following the second world war, we find the increasing influence of American tradition of village studies as reflected in the book by Ryan (Bryce Ryan *et al.*, 1958), and the historical tradition in American Cultural Anthropology as in Ralph Piers' work (1956). S.J. Tambiah's study of Polyandry with special reference to the Laggala Region in Ceylon, however, refers to the use of Leach's model of Kinship studies. With several case studies collected from Laggala villages and with the help of numerous genealogies, Tambiah, a native anthropologist trained at Cambridge, examines the impact of new values in marriage form and the governmental laws. He goes to establish that despite the legal form, numerous instances confirm the customary type of Polyandry (1966 : 319).

Nepal

Among those who have carried on vigorous and extensive field work in Nepal, C. von Furer-Haimendorf is the only significant name. In addition to publishing a large number of papers, Haimendorf published an ethnographic monograph on the Sherpas of Nepal (Haimendorf : 1964) and edited a volume on the *Caste and Kin in Nepal, India and Ceylon* (1966). His book, *Morals and Merits* also deals in part, with the Hindu customs and values which remained, by and large, unexposed to the Western influences (Haimendorf: 1967). In his edited volume, Haimendorf contributes two valuable papers : one on the unity and diversity in the Chetri Caste, and the other on caste concepts and status distinction in Buddhist communities of Western Nepal. In the first paper in the light of Chetri caste study, he endeavours to make a clear-cut distinction between caste and class status, because the some endogamous group comprises an immensely rich and until recently powerful aristocracy, a middle class, the peasantry and even landless families of working class status. In his second paper, with Colin Rosser (1966), he examines the pattern of co-existence and harmonisation caused in Nepal where Hindu and Buddhist civilisations meet and merge.

In addition to Haimendorf's work, an American anthropologist, John T. Hitchcock (1966) did intensive field work among the Magars of Banyan hills. The Japanese scholars have also been interested in multi-disciplinary study of Nepal under the auspices of Fauna and Flora Research Institute of Kyoto University. Out of several volumes of publications resulting out of the Japanese expedition in 1952, volume III edited by H. Kihar (1957) is devoted to the culture of the people of Nepal. The volume provides rich and factual ethnographic details of the tribes and castes of Nepal.

Indian anthropologists of late have also evinced some interest in the study of their neighbouring countries. (M. Jha : 1971), for example, disintensive field work in the pilgrim town of Janakpur in Nepal, and using the methodological lead given in *The Sacred Complex of Gaya* (Vidyarthi : 1961) he described the Sacred Complex of Janakpur. Another Indian sociologist, Gopal Singh Nepali (1965) made an ethno-sociological study of the Newar in Nepal.

Though Anthropology has been recognized as an important discipline in Nepal, and though for his outstanding work in Nepal the British anthropologist Haimendorf was given by the King of Nepal, the highest honour of the country the teaching and research in Anthropology is yet to be organized at the University level.

5 Anthropology in South-East Asia, Japan and Far-East

Anthropology in South-East Asia

TILL the end of the second world war, anthropological researches in South-East Asia also were under the influence of the colonial tradition of the British and other European countries. After the war, however, the climate changed in favour of American Anthropology and, in the absence of native scholars, most of the field researches and publications till mid-'sixties, were by the American and other West European scholars. In a couple of survey papers, Donald J. Tugby (1968) and Elise Tugby (1968) present a statistical appraisal of ethnological and allied work on South-East Asia conducted during the period 1950-1966.

It is reported that since 1950, 182 workers have made 305 field trips to South-East Asia and 332 field visits to individual countries. The most researched country in South-East Asia is Thailand, which has absorbed 26.8% of all field visits. Other heavily researched countries are the Philippines (19.6%), Indonesia (16.3%) and Malaysia (14.8%). The other major countries of South-East Asia, Burma, Cambodia, Laos and the two Vietnams have had only 19.9% of all field visits, representing an average of about one visit per year to each country.

When viewed from the place of origin of field workers, 47.9% of all field visits were made by the workers from the United States, 21.7% by workers from Europe, 13% by workers from Australia-Japan and 17.5% by workers from South-East Asia itself. Since the total research efforts of the United States is the largest, it is worth a second look. The percentages of the total number of field visits from the United States in the major countries of research are as follows : the Philippines (28.3%), Thailand (24.5%), Malaysia (15.1%) and Indonesia (13.3%). It confirms the impression that the United States dominates research in these countries.

Of 354 research topics reported, the major topics are in Ethnography (78.0%) followed by Linguistics (11.3%), Archaeology and Cultural History (7.9%), Demography (1.4%) and Music (0.8%). Great majority of topics invested by the workers from the United States and Australia-Japan are in the field of Ethnography (84.5% and 97.6% respectively). Ethnographic projects, however, are less popular among workers from Europe and South-East Asia. They are replaced by the linguistic projects among European workers, and the archaeological projects among South-East Asian workers.

The topical approach reveals national and regional differences in the styles of work. According to an analysis of the questionnaires made by Tugby, European and South-East Asian workers place more emphasis on diachronic studies, partly because of their ethnological traditions and partly because of their interests in their own (pre-colonial) culture. The ethno-historical approach is still dominant in Germany. Australian workers use the functional-structural model and the Japanese workers use more descriptive ethnographic model. The US anthropologists, however, follow analytic style such as ecological, psychological interactional and such other anthropological models of American Anthropology.

On the basis of their prolonged field work varying in range from one year to seven months, workers from Europe put in 12.2 months; from United States, 14.3 months; Australia-Japan, 7.9 months; South-East Asian workers, 7 months. These workers studied different types of field problems and published several papers, books, reports, notes, etc.

At the South-East Asian level certain generalized pictures regarding Ecology (L.G. Loffler : 1963), Economy and Religion (K. Itawa : 1965) and ritual symbols (F.R. Vonder Mendon : 1963) and the model of South-East Asian Society (M. Nash :

1964) have been published. Several symposia were held on the South-East Asian level and a Journal of South-East Asian studies has started publication since 1962. The South-East Asian area study and research programmes were organised in several universities in the United States. The Institute of Ethnography in USSR and Australian universities in their limited way also emphasized the study of South-East Asia and Pacific islands. All these led to exchange of scholars and students in a big way in spite of the fact that the visa entry remained difficult and time-consuming in some countries.

Anthropology in the Philippines

In terms of the national level, the Philippines, as observed earlier, attracted more foreign scholars and the number of anthropological institutions grew rapidly in cities like Quezon (6), Manila (5), Gagayadero (4), Cebu (4), and Dumaguete (4). A few national journals, namely, *Silliman Journal, Practical Anthropology*, etc. were published from Philippines. Under the Area Research Programmes of the Chicago University, Fred Eggan (1963) made valuable contributions by (*1*) setting a model for research and publication, and (*2*) preparing the Philippines' scholars to undertake anthropological researches in the country. Conklin's own contributions to the anthropological study in Philippines have been quite varied ranging from ethno-ecological studies (1954-1959) to linguistic studies (1955, 1956), and work on folklore and music. Some scholars took up sociological researches of inter-group relationship and social organizations among the Muslims (R. Stone : 1962), while others concentrated on the Chinese migrants (G.W. Skiner : 1951). The other American trends such as village and community studies, psychological researches found adequate recognition in Cultural Anthropology in the Philippines.

Anthropology in Thailand

The hill tribes in Thailand were of special interest to foreign scholars who studied them with a view to solving the problem of national development. A tribal research centre at Chiengwai in North-Western Thailand was established and several publications were brought out by the Department of Public Welfare at Bangkok (H. Manndorff: 1962, 1964). American scholars (P. Kunsdatter : 1966; F.M. Lebar *et. al*: 1964) wrote on the several ethnic groups of Thailand. With assistance from Cornell University, village studies were also undertaken (L.C. Judd : 1954; R.W. Kickert : 1960). The studies of this personality structure also attracted the attention of psychologically-oriented anthropologists (K.M. Hanks and H.Phillip: 1961). W.G. Skiner made a comparative study of Chinese society in Thailand (1957, 1964). Sociological analysis of *Bangkhuad* was published by an American scholar, Kauffman (1962). Even the US Information Service undertook pilot village studies in certain parts of Thailand (R.W. Kickert : 1960). A few Japanese scholars (K. Itawa : 1964; Obayashi : 1964) described the rural society of Thailand.

Though the anthropological researches that have attracted the Western and Asian scholars go to establish the importance of Thailand as an anthropologically important nation, the native infra-structure for such work, however, is very weak as only one anthropological institution is located in the country. The political situations also hamper the outsiders from working smoothly. It becomes national responsibility to generate local skill to undertake anthropological enquiry in the light of local needs and, hopefully, locally valid and generated models.

Anthropology in Indonesia

Different Indonesian islands, rich as they are in the archaeological and anthropological materials owing to their prolonged contacts with India, have been of special attraction for research to the Western, specially the Dutch and Norwegian scholars. After the second world war, however, the American Anthropology has considerably influenced researches in this area. Skinner organized a symposium on Village Indonesia and published the proceedings (1959) which include papers on different aspects of Indonesian Island villages. He also published a report on the Chinese in South-East Asia (1951) including Indonesia which was followed by a long paper on the Chinese in Indonesia published in a book on Indonesia, edited by McVey (1963).

In addition to numerous studies on Indonesia there have

been scholars specializing on different islands and on different themes. Among these scholars, the numbers of theoretically oriented and methodologically sophisticated publications of C.J. Geertz deserve special mention. Geertz's chief interest had been in the study of religious beliefs and practices in Jawa (1956, 1959, 1960). He has also contributed immensely to the understanding of Japanese economy, and his chief publication has been in relation to the process of ecological change in Indonesia in relation to agriculture (Geertz : 1963).

The study of Bali, again, was taken up by several scholars establishing the Hindu-Balinese religious continuum (C. Hooykaas : 1963, 1964; R.P. Soejono : 1961). Mead and Bateson made a study of the Balinese culture in the light of their culture personality school (G. Bateson and M. Mead : 1942).

In view of the increased contact of the native scholars, firstly with the Dutch and then with the American and other western scholars the native interest in Anthropology is on the increase. Several anthropological institutions have come up in Djakarta (4), Bandung (5) and Jog Jakaria (2). Some of the native scholars are engaged in self-study and have become critical of studies by others.

Anthropology in Malaysia

Malaysia has been the country of anthropological interests to many leading British and American anthropologists. R. Needham made valuable contributions to the study of kinship system on the basis of his field studies of the Penan of North Borneo (1953, 1955A, 1955B). M.G. Swift studied Malayan culture from economic, political and social angles and presented an analytical picture of Malayan culture (1962, 1964, 1965). The agricultural practices and family system of the Iban have been the major themes of research of D. Freeman in Borneo (1955, 1957). An Indian anthropologist, R.K. Jain under the influence of British social anthropologists made the study of one rubber plantation, Pal Melaya, where the South Indian labourers not only produce rubber for export, but lead their whole life, *i.e.*, grow up, marry, save, and consume, quarrel and cooperate, and die. (Jain : 1970)

The less studied South-East Asian nations are Burma,

Cambodia, Laos and the two Vietnams. Burma which has been the centre for anthropological research by Leach and other British anthropologists in the post war period were studied by several American scholars. Manning Nash (1963, 1964) and his wife J. Nash (1966) studied the various aspects of Burmese Buddhism as practised in everyday life, as well as marriage, family and population growth in upper Burma.'E.M. Mendolson (1960, 1963, 1965) brought out a series of publication on the Burmese practice of Buddhism and the Burmese establishment. The work of M. Spiro on Burmese religious behaviour is also a commendable piece of work (Spiro : 1967). The structure of Chin society was studied by F.K. Lehman (1963) who presented a dynamic picture of a community adapted to a non-Western civilization.

Among a few publications on Cambodia, mention may be made of the researches of the Japanese scholars, N. Matsumoto (1959, 1965) and of K. Iwata (1959) on the ethnic groups of Laos. A few American scholars including H.K. Kauffman, who worked on the Laos project sponsored by the University of California, made several village studies (1962).

In Vietnam, in addition to publication of a few American scholars (H.K. Kauffman : 1963, L.C. Thompson : 1959) a few Soviet anthropologists from the Institute of Ethnography at Moscow conducted field work and made publication in their journal, *Soviet Ethnography*. Among these scholars, mention may be made of Aroutiounov and Boriskowski of Moscow and of Dementiev and Muklinov of Leningrad who did ethnological and archaeological researches in Vietnam during the period under review.

Anthropology in Japan

Following a trade treaty with the Western nations in 1859 by the Takugawa Government and by lifting of the legal ban against Christianity in 1872 by the Meiji Government, Japan was in a position to initiate international relations with the world (Sumiya, Mikio : MSS : 1968). Contacts in the field of Anthropology, however, remained almost absent till the beginning of the third-quarter of this century.

A few researches on Japanese culture were conducted before

the second world war. Among them the much-debated book is by Ruth Benedict (1946) on the Japanese national character. A special number of the *Japanese Journal of Ethnology* (1949) was devoted to the problems raised in this book. On the whole, considering the author's lack of field work in Japan, the book has found acceptance among Japanese ethnologists, only with the comment that the detailed explanations of Japanese culture therein were quite removed from their standard.

Another book on Japanese national character was by Gorer (1943) which is considered as one-sided and devoid of accurate interpretation. Babree's *Suye Mura* is considered an excellent work on a Japanese village, and it marks the American influence of village studies in Japan (Embree : 1946). These sporadic Western contacts could not, however, make much influence in the development of Japanese Anthropology. Eiichin Ishida, participating in the International Anthropological Symposium of the Wenner Gren Foundation in 1952, has dwelt on the poor state of Japanese anthropology. He observes :

> Japanese anthropology began late, and is still in its infancy. Its contemporary status can be summarised as lacking in balance and in integration of its fields. No Japanese university has yet an independent department of anthropology, and archaeology, linguistics etc. These are offered as isolated courses in some host departments. (E. Ishida : 1953 : 342-43).

During the post-war period, after the wounds caused by the atomic war were partly healed, the Japanese Anthropology showed phenomenal growth. According to Ishida, three distinct features marked Japanese Anthropology in the post-war periods: They are (*1*) the collapse of the militaristic regime which freed Japanese Anthropology of the long-imposed taboo on speaking any truth which might contradict the conception of divine origin of the imperial family; (*2*) the broadening of the interest in studying the ethnic origins and native customs of the Japanese; and (*3*) the birth of the realisation to develop integrated anthropological sciences. The widespread recognition of this need is evidenced by the formation in 1948 of a league for the study of human affairs. Among the urgent needs in Japanese Anthropology, Ishida emphasized the use of establishing independent departments of Anthropology in some major Japanese Universities with balanced representation of fields.

With the dynamic leadership given by senior colleagues in the profession, particularly by E. Ishida and M. Oka, Japanese Anthropology developed at an accelerated speed. In the 'fifties and 'sixties, a few of the Japanese scholars learnt foreign languages and some of them came to German, American, British and Indian Universities and Institutes for advanced training and research. Out of them, mention may be made of Yoshiro Shiratori who went to Vienna and was trained in German school of Ethnology. Chie Nakane came to India and was attached to Anthropological Survey of India and did her initial field work under the guidance of Dr. B.S. Guha, who was himself trained at Harvard. Later, she made frequent visits and a prolonged stay at an advanced centre of learning in America. From time to time several Japanese scholars went to different American Universities under the Fulbright and other American Foundations' programmes.

With these increasing contacts, contemporary Japanese Anthropology reflects greater influence of American Anthropology and in four universities (Tokyo, Meije, Nagoa and Osaka) the post-graduate and research instructions have been organized on a sounder footing. In addition, Anthropology is being taught in several colleges at the under-gruduate level, and it also constitutes a part of the curriculum of the disciplines of social sciences, particularly Sociology, Archaeology and languages.

A big jump in Japanese Anthropology came with the holding of the Eighth International Congress of Anthropological and Ethnological Sciences at Tokyo and Kyoto. Earlier the hosting by Japan of the Eleventh Pacific Science Congress in 1966 at Tokyo also prepared a healthy ground for anthropological expedition. In addition to receiving support from foundations, universities and institutes some of the Japanese business and industrial firms, Railway company, etc., also came forward to finance anthropological expeditions. Television and film companies also displayed increasing interest in bringing nearer home the exotic life and culture of the tribes of the Pacific Islands and the deep forests and deserts of Africa and South America. Anthropologists were invited to help in producing films on the tribes of obscure areas, including one on the

Eskimos which was undertaken by Dr. Masao Oka, the past president of the Eighth International Congress of Anthropological and Ethnological Sciences. The Nagea Railway Company, for the purposes of tourism, established an open air museum at Nagoa ('The Little World Museum of Man') which is in the process of expansion. At Osako, with the assistance of the National Government, an open air museum is under construction.

With all these favourable factors and forces Japanese Anthropology has taken considerable strides forward, during the last 25 years. A large number of anthropological institutions have been established in different parts of the country. In Tokyo alone, according to Fifth International Directory of Anthropologists, the number of anthropological centres come to 70. Several anthropological institutions are located in Kyoto (8), Nagoa (5), Osaka (4), Inuyama (4), Fukuoka-chi (3), Kumanotoshi (3), and Sapporo (3). The Directory lists 224 anthropologists and estimates 300 anthropologists in the Far East, who evidently are mainly from Japan.

By and large the anthropological researches conducted by the Japanese have been reported in Japanese language. Their journals are published by the two major anthropological societies: (*i*) by the Japanese Society of Anthropology (of which Prof. Hisashi Suzuki of Tokyo University is the President) and (*ii*) by the Japanese Society of Ethnology (of which Prof. Masao Gomo of Maize University is the President). There are a few other journals of anthropological nature which are also published in the Japanese language. Japanese scholars have also published their research findings in book form in their own language. However, they are, also familiar with the literature published in foreign languages particularly in English, and some of the scholars have translated important books by the British and American anthropologists into Japanese. In this regard special mention may be made of Dr. Monkichi Namba who has translated into Japanese Evans Pritchard's *Social Anthropology* (1957) and Clyde Kluckhohn's *Concept of Culture* (1948).

Among those who have written profusely in English, mention may be made of Chie Nakane who is currently Professor at the Institute of Oriental Culture in the University of Tokyo. Nakane's publications are mainly based on her field work in Sikkim, Assam, West Bengal and Kerala. Her manifold exposure to British and American Anthropology has encouraged her on the one hand to take up studies on kinship, and the matrilineal system, on the other, to take up village studies. Owing to short spell of field work, Nakane has not been very rich and exhaustive, but even then her writings on India reflect the Japanese view points, which are different from those of the Western scholars (1966, 1967A, 1967B).

Nakane's studies of the Japanese society (1967C, 1970, 1972) are also valuable contributions to Japanese Anthropology. In the background of her broad field experience in the study of both Asian and Western countries, she interprets the structure of Japanese society in the books published both in Japanese (Tateshakai No Ningen Kankei : 1967) and in English (*Japanese Society* : 1970). From the study of this book it becomes clear that the Western model even applied by the Japanese scholars could not explain the elements of Japanese social structure; Nakane proposes a set of new theories, concepts, and terms to understand the Japanese reality. It is a great step forward. It establishes the general need for formulating a set of new theories and methodology for understanding a tradition bound-society like Japan. Her approach in these books is a pointer to the fact that theories or models evolved through studies dealing mainly with Western societies, and undertaken by Western scholars, hurriedly fall short in explaining the tradition-bound, historical and complex societies of the oriental countries. It also establishes the fact that indigenous theories and methods need to be evolved to understand the complexity of their own societies.

The Ainu tribe of Hokkaido, like Vedda of Ceylon or the Toda of South India have attracted foreign scholars since the nineteenth century (J. Batchelor : 1805, 1901, and B.D. Howard : 1893). The interests of some of Japanese scholars in studying the dynamics of Ainu Culture of the Hokkaido Island continued though during the Tokyo Congress both the papers on Ainu were presented by American scholars (Carl Schusterl : 1968 and Chestor S. Chard : 1968). The exploration club of Hokkaido University, Sapporo, originally established for field work among the Ainus, and the northern centre of Japanese research continue to take interest in ethnographic studies under the guidance of local ethnologist, Tetsure Swane.

Along with the Ainus the north Asian nomads have also

been of considerable interest to the Japanese Ethnologists. Originally they conducted historical, archaeological and linguistic researches. However in contemporary time, the study of modern nomands have generated considerable interests. Nameo Egami (1968) has conducted similar research on the origin of nomadism in Mongolia.

Some sociologically oriented anthropologists have gone beyond historical and ethnological interests and have studied the processes of urbanization and its manifold modernising impacts. Takeshi Ishida, for example, worked on urbanization and its impact on Japanese politics (1966). Summing up he suggests: "the pattern of urbanization in all the late and rapidly developing countries, there occurs a social and cultural lag and feeling of anti-urbanization." He makes the appraisal of Japanese urbanization under the theoretical influence of Karl Mannheim (1943, 1957). He also draws heavily for facts on a paper written by Robert E. Ward (1965) an American political sociologist.

Again, under the influence of an American scholar, Koichi Niitsu (1968) of Rikkyo University, he makes a study of the process of change from rural to urban values. He draws his samples from among the Asian students coming from rural areas of Japan, Thailand and the Philippines and presents a cross-cultural study statistically.

The modern sociological themes concerning the contemporary Japanese society are also being studied by the government-sponsored institution of Statistical Mathematics in the Ministry of Education and Public Relations section of Prime Minister's office. These researches use sophisticated tools of statistical analysis. The Japanese national character, for example, which was earlier studied by Ruth Benedict and followed by several Japanese scholars, found a statistical analysis by the Institute of Statistical Mathematics. The opinions expressed by a great majority of the Japanese regarding their national character are as follows:

> They are satisfied with the present; religious teaching is important, but they do not believe in religion. Men must behave the way the text-book of pre-war moral education taught; they respect "theie" (or the traditional Japanese family system and ancestors); they are tolerant of others, they

favour a paternalistic boss even if he is irrational; they admire success in life, as was the case of Hideyoshi, Ruler of Japan in the sixteenth century; they prefer to be born males; they think married women should be engaged only in keeping houses; they prefer hobby and style of life which are traditionally Japanese. (Report : 1961)

Similarly, the Prime Minister's office published sophisticated reports on even themes like contentment towards life, class structure etc., with adequate statistical sophistication. For these researches, trained social scientists are employed who apply the questionnaire method borrowed mainly from American Sociology.

Of late the Japanese anthropologists have taken up field expedition and researches outside Japan. Their main areas of interests are the neighbouring islands of Far East, South-Eastern Asia and also Oceania. Michio Suenari (1968) has made a theory-oriented study of kinship among the Puyuma of Taiwan. The highland tribes of New Guinea has been studied by Sachiko Hatanaka (1968), and Yoshiro Shiratori. Vienna trained Professor at Sofia University published several papers on the ethnic groups of South-East Asia (1966).

In other islands of the Far East, along with the economic aid from Japan, the Japanese scholars have been able to influence anthropological development. Among the native scholars of Far East, mention may be made of Dushyan Lee of Seoul National University (1968); Chang Chung (1968) of the Museum of Korean folklore, who have been interested on some aspects of Korean religion and myths; and Kawang-Kyu Lee (1968) of Seoul National University, who has published on matrilineal phenomenon in ancient Korea.

Anthropology in Oceania

The three Oceanic Islands Melanesia, Polynesia and Micronesia have been the subject of research primarily by the British, German and American scholars. With foreign aid these Islands have long been exposed to foreign anthropologists. On account of the increasing facilities of air travel and grants for research, the Pacific Islands have been greatly accessible over the past fifty years. The classical anthropological interest initiated by British anthroplogist, W.H.R. Rivers, and followed by Malinowski and his students including Raymond Firth, then by several American scholars including Margaret Mead, Cora Dubois and others, evidently generated considerable anthropological study and literature. Australian social anthropologists mainly working under British influence also joined the rush for the study of the Oceanic tribes. The Australian Institute of Aboriginese Studies set up by the Government of Australia in 1961, specially the Australian National University established at Canberra, further intensified tribal researches in the Pacific Islands. In addition, Micronesia has also been studied by the prehistorians and linguists. A review of prehistoric research has been published by Peter Bellwood (1978) in *Current Anthropology.*

The Oceanian culture has undergone considerable transformation at an accelerated speed during the last two-quarters of this century. Mead, who wrote about Samoan and the Manus in late 'twenties and 'thirties was inspired to re-study their 'New lives for Old' in 1956 (M. Mead : 1956). Making a case for the urgency of ethno-musicological research, Wolfgang Laade (1970) complains that "all traces of the indigenous culture, had long since disappeared."

The Western anthropologists have been able to follow up the transformation scene, but the native initiatives have remained completely absent. The University of Papua and New Guinea (1965) and the University of the South Pacific (1968) have been established and local students are being taught by the staff recruited internationally. These universities are likely to throw in local talents for 'self study', including the impact of accelerated tempo of Westernisation in Oceania.

6 | Conclusion

IT gets established, thus, that the last quarter of this century has been the most productive period in the history of World Anthropology. Anthropology, as a science of man and his culture, has been a witness to an accelerated proliferation and diversification in the development of sub-fields and topics. While the older theories and methods have persisted in a modified form, along with them the newer ones have also further contributed to the expansive nature of development. In its expansion, inter-disciplinarity and choice of topics, the only limiting factor, it seems, has been 'man'. In view of all these developments, Stanley Diamond (1964 : 433) terms it a revolutionary discipline; "a modern metaphysics, a science of sciences that may inquire into the nature of history of man, for the sake of man and in his name."

To some, so much diversification has been a matter of worry as it may bring about the extinction of Anthropology as a discipline. Such fear, however, is unfounded, as eclecticism has been the basic strength of Anthropology. This science of man traditionally owes its origin to a 'science without portfolio', or as Levi-Strauss puts it a 'garbage' of other disciplines.

The period, under review, is also noted for the liberation of several colonial countries and their increasing contacts with America. This accelerated the post-war tradition of a switch over from the colonial temper of Commonwealth and West

European Anthropology to informal trends of American Anthropology. A smooth transition could be specially possible because of America's increased resources, discovery of new instruments of research and theoretical models, and, above all, an effective use of numerous media of communication (internationa l symposia, *Current Anthropology*, *World Journal*, etc.).

In view of all these developments, American Anthropology acquired undisputed leadership in the field of the science of man and his culture. This process leading to monopolistic situation continued almost undisturbed till the mid-'sixties when the over-Americanization of theory, method and field expeditions were resented, as it fell short in explaining the complexities of the traditional societies like India, Japan and South-East Asia. To some, the Americanization was so dominant and overwhelming that it was considered as a switch over from colonial Anthropology to neo-colonial or Imperial Anthropology.

In the context of Indian Sociology and Anthropology, Gore (M.S. Gore : N.D.) refers to this ambivalence towards America, and observes that it hinges not only on our approach to American Social Sciences but nearly every thing American. Those educated in the British Universities were sceptical about what American scholarship offered. Other criticism of American Scholars is based on an assumption of superficiality, inadequate field work and indiscriminate application of the questionnaire technique. Those who have found American influence useful refer to the growing sophistication of research methodology, the use of new concepts and terms as tools of analysis, the diversification of research interest and introduction and spread of theoretical models.

N.K. Bose, making a plea for the decolonization of Indian Anthropology, writes :

> The position of Indian Anthropology has on the whole been colonial in relation to schools which have dominated the European or American scene from time to time. (Bose : 1963 : 46)

A few scholars trained in America complain : "Many of us still publish to gain approvals of our patrons and mentors in the

West." (G. Sarana and D.P.Sinha 1976 : 219). Another anthropologist feels, perhaps in the light of his own experience, the need to inquire the extent to which Academic patronage and linkages with the western *Guru* (teacher) and *Gurubhai* (disciples of the same teacher) continue to be a decisive factor in shaping the contour of a scholarly enterprise in Anthropology in India today. (S.C. Sinha : 1971).

In spite of their scientific interest, the constraints of foreign scholars in studying 'other cultures' have been pointed out both by Indian and Japanese scholars. When a foreigner comes to study the complexity of India, he brings with him the concepts and theoretical framework as well as research procedures developed by western anthropologists in their study of simple non-literate and relatively homogeneous and isolated communities that are quite unlike those in complex India (Gopala Sarana and D.P. Sinha : 1976 : 215). Similarly, Chie Nakane finds the use of the western model inadequate for understanding the Japanese society. To her, "the application of western theories to Japanese society may be likened to the use of the metric system in taking the standard measurements of Japanese clothes." She refers to the disservice done even by the Japanese anthropologists, who dispose of their indigenous phenomena, that did not fit in with western theories, precisely by labelling them as Japan's 'feudal' or 'backward' elements—a very convenient solution. (Chie Nakane : 1972 : 2).

Recent reactions of the central European national ethnographer towards American Anthropology have already been referred to scholars like Hultkrantz (1965) and Hofer (1968) who have openly declared that a wholesale adaptation of American Anthropology would be a backward step as it suffers from several shortcomings, from which 'national ethnography' is happily free.

The survey also reflects that, though the American model of anthropology has found great 'Universalization', a national pattern of the pre-war period persists with certain adaptations and additions. In this respect the retention of the 'national or regional ethnography', as it has been recently termed by the central European countries, has been the most distinguishing feature. While Canada, South America, Oceania and South-

East Asia have largely absorbed American trends, other countries like India and Australia have not only retained the traditions of Commonwealth Anthropology but also borrowed theories, methods, and techniques from American Anthropology.

Issues regarding the values involved in studying 'others' culture' and the natives' reaction to undergo such studies have come for careful ethical scrutiny. In some cases excessive interventions have led to the loss of credibility of the anthropologists as field scientists.

In the field of theory, the greatest theoretical innovation since 1952 is the structuralism of Levi-Strauss. It has affected the community of scholars throughout the world. The anthropological theory of studying civilization in terms of 'traditions' proposed by Redfield and his colleagues in Chicago has found favourable acceptance by workers in Asia and elsewhere.

While anthropology has retained its basic character to be a field science mainly based on 'micro approach' and 'participation', there has been considerable shift from the study of simpler societies or tribal research to complex and national societies. A change over from the descriptive, ethnographic or functional approach to inter-disciplinary, analytic and model-building trends is quite remarkable. This has made anthropology less 'provincial' and has made inter disciplinary co-operation more feasible.

It has further made anthropologists more conscious of methodology. They are becoming more and more aware of the need to discuss the epistemology and logic behind their empirical researches.

The use of statistics, however, continues to be the minimum. Except its use in Physical anthropological research, cross-cultural and large scale surveys, the use of statistics can be counted on fingers. With the growth of mathematical model, however, the quantitative approach in anthropology may gain ground, but its possibility in South Asia is rather remote where the extended spell of field research on micro units is still preferred.

The American and Japanese anthropologists make profuse use of mechanical and electrical goods to record the interviews, take photographs, and produce meticulous ethnographic films.

The ethnographic films which are screened during the world congresses on the life and culture of the natives of the remotest and most isolated areas evidence the use of technological development in the documentation of vanishing ethnographic data.

Appendix I

Notes

1. Dr. Rokkan, President of the ISSC raised the five questions to be responded by each disciplinary rapporteur. These questions are interrelated and interdependent and were replied to in a wholiestic manner. The questions were :

(i) Which theoretical innovations have left the heaviest impact on the discipline since 1952 and how have these affected the internationalisation of the discipline ?

(ii) What changes have occurred at the boundaries of the discipline and how have these affected interdisciplinary co-operation ?

(iii) What changes in methodology and technology have had the strongest impact on the internationalisation of activities ?

(iv) What has happened to the infrastructure for international co-operation over these years and how have these affected developments in the discipline ?

(v) What changes have occurred in the geographical reach of each discipline and which 'strategies for universalization' have proved most effective ?

2. Anthropology Today : An Encyclopaedic Inventory prepared under the chairmanship of A.L. Kroeber in 1952 with contributions from 52 writers basically reflects the status of American Anthropology at that time. Thirty-nine contributors were from America, two were trained in America and the remaining 11 were from other countries, particularly Great Britain, France, Germany etc.

The second volume published under the title *An Appraisal of Anthropology Today*, edited by Sol Tax and others is a springboard for talk about the future of Anthropology. It also provides the views of at least 25 participants from other parts of the world, their image of Anthropology, though about two-thirds of the participants were American. The first volume is a summary of what is known as American Anthropology in and around 1952. The second volume is a synthesis of what the American anthropologists expcet to find out in the future, and how other anthropologists look at them.

3. "The world view of any individual is a set of very wide range vectors in that individuals belief space (*a*) that he learned early in life and that are not readily changed and (*b*) that have a determinant influence on much of his observable behaviour both verbal and non-verbal, but (*c*) that he seldom or never verbalises in the referential mode, though (*d*) they are constantly conveyed by him as the expressive mode and as latent meanings."

4. These Departments offering Master's degrees are under the University of Calcutta 1920, Delhi 1947, Lucknow 1951, Ranchi 1953, Saugar 1954, Gauhati 1956, Utkal, Bhubaneshwar 1958, Karnatak (Dharwar 1959), Punjab (Chandigarh 1960), Andhra Pradesh (Waltair 1961), Ravishankar (Raipur 1965), Gujarat Vidyapith (Ahmedabad 1965), Dibrugarh (1966), Punjab (Patiala 1969), Poona (1969), Tirupati (1970), and Madras (1976).

Appendix II

Number of Books and Papers published on selected topics of Social and Cultural Anthropology

Countries	*Ethnography*		*Social Structure*		*Religion, Magic Witchcraft*		*Folk tradition*		*Acculturation and Social Change*		*Total*	
	Books	*Papers*	*Books*	*Papers*	*Books*	*Papers*	*Books*	*Papers*	*Books*	*Papers*	*Books*	*Papers*
Africa	46	23	19	42	11	42	21	32	21	44	118	183
America	63	50	6	26	13	5	8	18	23	39	113	168
Asia	21	14	4	14	8	26	2	13	8	19	43	86
Europe	11	15	2	11	4	18	9	26	11	14	37	84
Middle East	6	6	1	20	1	3	2	9	3	6	13	44
Pacific	30	17	4	19	3	13	2	13	11	17	50	79
USSR	34	10	3	17	1	35	6	25	6	24	50	111

Source : ICSSD International Bibliography of Social Sciences, Vol. XX, 1974.

References

Abbi, B.L. and Satis Saberwal (ed.) : *Urgent Anthropological Researches in India*, Simla, Indian Institute of Advanced Study, 1969.

Aiyappan, A : "Nayar Polyandry" in *Man*, 32(99), 1932, pp. 78-79.

——. "Caste and Joint Family in Tamil Nadu" in *Sociological Bulletin*, 4(2), 1955, pp. 117-122.

Averkiyeva, Y.P. : "Neo-Evolutionism and Modern American Ethnography" in *Soviet Ethnography*, No. 6, 1959.

——. "Neo-Evolutionism, Relativism and Racialism" in *Races and People* : Contemporary Ethnic and Racial Problems (ed.), Moscow, Progress Publishers, 1974, pp. 306-320.

Ayabe, T. : "The Concept of the 'Corn Spirit' on the Mainland of South-east Asia" in *Social Anthropology*, 2(3), 1965.

Bailey, F.G. : *Caste and the Economic Frontier*, London, Oxford University Press, 1958.

——. *Tribe, Caste and Nation*, Oxford and Manchester, Oxford University Press, 1960.

Banton, Michael (ed.) : *The Relevance of Models for Social Anthropology*, London, Tavistock Publications, 1965.

——. *Political Systems and the Distribution of Power*, London, Tavistock Publications, 1965.

——. *The Social Anthropology of Complex Societies*, London, Tavistock Publications, 1966.

Barth, F. : *Principles of Social Organisation in Southern Kurdistan*, Oslo, Brodrence Jorgenson A/S Boktrykkeri, 1953.

——. "The System of Social Stratification in Swet, North Pakistan" in *Aspects of Caste in Northern-West Pakistan* ed. E.R. Leach, Cambridge, Cambridge University Press, 1960.

Barthes, Ronald : "The Structuralist Activity", trans. Richard Howard in Richard T. De George and Fernande M. De George, eds. *The Structuralists from Marx to Levi-Strauss*, Anchor Book ed., Garden City, New York, Double-day and Co., 1972.

Barnet, Homer, G. : *Innovation*, New York, McGraw-Hill Book Co., 1953.

Batchelor, J. : *The Ainu of Japan*, New York, 1895.

——. *The Ainu and their Folklore*, London, The Religious Tract Society, 1901.

Bateson, G. and M. Mead : *Balinese Character : A Photographic Analysis* special publication of New York Academy of Sciences, 2, New York, New York Academy of Science, 1942.

Beech, Mary Jane, P.J. Bertocci and A. Corvin : "Introducing the East Bengali village" in *Inside the East Pakistan village —Six Articles*, Asian Studies Papers reprints series No. 2 (1965-1966), Asian Studies Centre, Michigan, Michigan State University, 1966.

Belshaw, Cyril S. : *The Conditions of Social Performance*, New York, Schoken Books, 1970.

Bellowood, Peter : "The Prehistory of Oceania" in *Current Anthropology*, vol. 16, No. 1, 1975, pp. 9-28.

Benedict, Ruth : *Patterns of Cultures*, New York, Houghton Mifflin, 1934.

——. *The Chrysanthemum and the Sword*, Boston, Noughton Miffin, 1946.

Berlin, Brent, Dennis, E. Breadlove & Peter H. Raven : "Convert Categories and Folk Taxonomias" in *American Anthropologist*, vol. 70, 1968, pp. 290-299.

Bhagbat, D. : *An outline of Indian Folklore*, Bombay, Popular Book Depot, 1958.

Bhowmick, P.K. : *The Lodhas of West Bengal* : (A Socio-economic Study), Calcutta, Punthi Pustak, 1963.

Bose, N.K. : "The Spring-Festival of India" in *Man in India*, vol. 7, 1927.

——. "Suggestions for Improvement in Methods" in *Presidential Address, Anthropology and Archaeology Section*, Indian Science Congress Association, Calcutta, 1949.

Bose, N.K. : "Introduction, Peasant Life in India" in *Anthropological Survey of India*, Memoir, No. 8, Calcutta, 1962.

——. "Fifty years of Science in India : Progress of Anthropology and Archaeology" in *Indian Science Congress Association*, Calcutta, 1963.

Bromley, Y.V. : "The term 'Ethnos' and its Definition" in I.R. Grigulevick and S.Y. Kozlov (eds.) *Races and Peoples*: Contemporary Ethnic and Racial Problems, Moscow, Progress Publishers, 1974, pp. 17-44.

Bromley, Y.V. and V.I. Kozlov : "National Processes in the USSR" in *Races and Peoples* : Contemporary Ethnic and Racial Problems, Moscow, Progress Publishers, 1974, pp. 116-138.

Bruner, E.M. : "The Toba Batak Village" in *Local, Ethnic and National Loyalties in village Indonesia* : *A symposium*, Edited by G.W. Skinner, South-east Asia Studies, Yale University, 1959.

——. "Urbanisation and ethnic identity in North Sumatra" in *American Anthropologist*, 63, 1961, pp. 508-521.

Brunk, S.I., N.N. Cheboksarov and Y.V. Chesnov : "National Processes in Asiatic Countries outside the USSR" in I.R. Grigulevion and S.Y. Kozlov (eds.), *Races and Peoples* : Contemporary Ethnic and Racial Problems, Moscow, Progress Publishers, 1974, pp. 182-211.

Burling, Robbins : *Renganggri*, Philadelphia, University of Pennsylvania Press, 1963.

Compell, Donald : "The Mutual Methodological Relevance of Anthropology and Psychology" in Francis Hsu, ed., *Psychological Anthropology* : Approaches to Culture and Personality, Homewood, 111, Dorsey Press, 1961, pp. 333-352.

Chapple, Eliot D. : *Culture and Biological Man*, New York, Holt. Richart and Winston, 1970.

Chapple, Eliot D. and Carleton S. Coon : *Principles of Anthropology*, New York, Henry Holt & Co., 1942.

Chard, Chester S. : "A New Look at the Ainu Problem" in *Proceedings of VIIIth ICAES*, vol. III, Tokyo & Kyoto, Science Council of Japan, 1968, pp. 98-99.

Chaudhuri, Dulal : "Methodology in Folklore Research and Archiving" in *Folklife* (Calcutta), 1973, pp. 17-21.

Cheboksaro, N.N. : "Problems of the origin of Ancient and Contemporary Peoples" Presented in the *VIIIth International Congress of Anthropological and Ethnological Sciences*, Moscow, 1964.

Chekki, D.A. : "Community Research in India : Some Trends" in *VIIIth World Congress of Sociology*, International Sociological Association, 1974.

Childe, V.G. : *Man Makes Himself*, New York, New American Library, 1942.

Choudhury, M.I. and M.A. Khan : *Pakistan Society : A Sociological Analysis*, Lahore, Noorsons, 1964.

Chugun, Chang : "Folkloric Study on the Korean Myths" in *Proceedings*, vol. II, VIIIth ICAES, Tokyo and Kyoto, Science Council of Japan, 1968, pp. 284-286.

Cipriani, Lideo : *The Andaman Islanders* (edited and translated by Taylor Cox), London, Weidenfield and Nicolson, 1969

Cohn, B.S. : *India : The Social Anthrapology of a Civilization*, Englewood Cliffs, New Jersey, Prentice-Hall Inc., 1971.

Conklin, H.C. : *An Ethnoecological approach to Shifting Agriculture*, Transactions of the New York Academy of Science, Series 2, 17(Reprinted in Readings in Cultural Geography, Edited by P.L. Wagner and M.W. Mikeseel, pp. 457-464, Chicago, University of Chicago Press, 1962), 1954, pp. 132-33

——. *Preliminary Linguistic Survey of Mindanao*, University of Chicago, Philippine Studies Program, 1955.

——. "Hanunoo music from the Philippine" in *Ethnic Folkways Library Album*, p. 466, 112' 33P/3RPM disk and program notes (Musical notes by Jose Maceda) New York, Folkways Records and Service Corporation, n.d.

——. "Tagolog disguised speech" in *Language*, 32, 1956, pp. 136-139.

——. "Ecological interpretations and plant domestication" in *American Antiquity* 25, 1959, 260-62.

Coughlin, R.J. : *South-east Asian birth, customs*, New Haveo : Human Relations Area Files Press, 1965.

Deva, Indra : "Folklore Studies" in *A Survey of Researches in Sociology and Social Anthropology*, vol. III, by ICSSR, Bombay, Popular Prakashan, 1972, pp. 197-239.

Dhillon, H.S. : *Leadership and Groups in a South Indian Village*, New Delhi, Planning Commission (PED Publication, No. 9), 1955.

Diomond, Stanley : "A Revolutionary Discipline" in *Current Anthropology*, vol. 5, 1964, pp. 432-437.

Douglas, Mary : *Natural Symbols*, London, Barrie and Rockliff, Cresset Press, 1970.

Dube, Leela : "Sociology of Kinship : A Trend Report" in *A Survey of Research in Sociology and Social Anthropology*, vol. II, ed. ICSSR, Bombay, Popular Prakashan, 1974, pp. 233-266.

Dube, S.C. : *Indian Village*, Ithaca, Cornell University Press, 1955.

——. "Approaches to the Tribal Problems" in *Indian Anthropology in Action* ed. by L.P. Vidyarthi, Ranchi, Council of Social and Cultural Research, Bihar, 1960.

——. "Social Anthropology in India" in *Indian Anthropology* : Essays in memory of D.N. Majumdar ed. by T.N. Madan and Gopala Sarana, Bombay, Asia Publishing House, 1962.

——. "Tribal Heritage of India", vol. I : *Ethnicity, Identity and Interaction*, New Delhi, Vikas Publishing House Pvt. Ltd., 1977.

Dumont, Louis : "Dravidian Kinship Terminology as an expression of Marriage," *Man*, 53(54), 1953.

——. Hierarchy and Marriage alliance in South Indian Kinship" in *Occasional Papers* No. (2), London, Royal Anthropological Institute, 1957.

Egami, Namio : "On the Origin of Nomadism in Mongolia" in *Proceedings of the VIIIth International Congress of Anthropological and Ethnological Sciences* (Ethnology and Archaeology), Tokyo and Kyoto, Science Council of Japan, 1968, p. 324.

Eggan, F. : "Social Anthropology and the Method of Controlled Comparison", *American Anthropologist* vol. 55, 1954, pp. 543-763.

—— : "Cultural drift and Social Change" in *Current Anthropology* 4, 1963, pp. 347-55.

Elwin, V. : *The Baiga*, London, John Murry, 1939.

Maria Murder and Suicide, London, Oxford University Press, 1943.

Elvin, V. : *The Aboriginals*, Bombay, Oxford University Press, 1943.

——. *Folktales of Mahakoshal*, Oxford University Press, 1944.

——. *The Muria and Their Ghotul*, Geoffery Camberlege, Oxford University Press, 1947.

——. *Tribal Myths of Orissa*, Oxford University Press, 1954.

——. *Religion of an Indian Tribe*, London, Oxford University Press, 1955.

——. *A Philosophy for NEFA*, Shillong, NEFA Administration, 1958.

——. *Tribal World of Verrier Elwin*, London, Oxford University Press, 1964.

Embree, John F. : Japanese village, London, 1946.

Evans Pritchard, E.E. : *The Nuer*, New York, Clarendon Press, 1940.

——. *Social Anthropology*, New York, Free Press, 1951.

Ferriera, J.V. : *Totemism in India*, Bombay, Oxford University Press, 1965.

Firth, Raymond : "Function" in *Current Anthropology : A Supplement of Anthropology Today* (ed.) W.L. Thomas, Jr. Chicago, The University of Chicago Press, 1955, pp. 237-258.

Fortes, Meyer : *Social Anthropology at Cambridge Since 1900, An Inaugural Lecture*, Cambridge, University Press, 1953.

Fox, Robin : "The Cultural Animal" in *Social Science Information*, vol. 9, 1970, pp. 7-25.

Frank, C.O. : "Sindangam Subanum Word List" in *Journal of East Asiatic Studies*, 3, 1956, pp. 321-324.

Frantz, Ch. : "The 20th Century Development of U.S. Anthropology : Universities, Government and the Private Sector" Prepared for the *Symposium* on "National Styles in the Development and Profession of Anthropology", 74th Annual Meeting, American Anthropological Association, San Francisco California, 6th December, 1975.

Freeman, D. : *Iban Agriculture*, London, Her Majesty's Stationery Office, 1955.

——. "The Family System of the Iban of Borneo" in *Cambridge Papers in Social Anthropology* No. 1, ed. by J. Goody, Cambridge, Cambridge University Press, 1957, pp. 15-52.

Fromm, Erich : "Psychoanalytic characterology and its application to the understanding of culture", in *Sargent and*

Smith, Culture and Personalities, New Haven, Yale University Press, 1950.

Fromm, Erich and Michal Maccoby : *Social Character in a Mexican Village*, Englewood Cliffs, N.J's. Prentice-Hall Inc., 1970.

Furer-Haimendorf C. von : *The Chenchus : The Jungle Folk of Deccan*, London, Macmillan & Co. 1943.

——. *Tribal Population of Hyderabad*, Hyderabad, Revenue Department (Census), 1945.

——. *The Reddis of Bison Hills : A Study in acculturation in Collaboration with Elizabeth* Von Furer-Haimendorf (in two vols.), London, Macmillan & Co., 1945.

——. *The Naked Nagas*, Calcutta (also Published from London, Macmillan & Co.), 1953.

——. *Himalayan Barbary*, London, John Murray, 1955.

——. *The Apa Tanis and Their Neighbours : A Primitive Civilization of the Eastern Himalayan*, London, Routledge and Kegan Paul, 1962.

——. *The Sherpas of Nepal : Buddhist Highlanders*, Berkeley & Los Angeles, University of California Press, 1964.

——. *Caste and Kin in Nepal, India and Ceylon*, Bombay, Asia Publishing House, 1966 (ed).

——. *Morals and Merits : A Study of Values and Social Controls in South Asian Societies*, London, Weidenfield and Nicolson, 1967.

Gankovsky, Yu V. : *The People of Pakistan : A Ethnic History*, Moscow, Nauka Publishing House, Central Department of Oriental Literature, 1971.

Geddes, W.R. : *The Hill Tribes of Thailand*, S.E.A.T.O. Record, September, 1965.

Geertz, C.J. Jr. : "Religious Beliefs and Economic Behaviour in a Central Javanese town : Some Preliminary Considerations", *Economic Development and Cultural Change*, 2, 1956, pp. 134-158.

——. "Form and Variation in Balinese Village Structure", *American Anthropologist*, vol. 61, 1959, pp. 991-1012.

——. *Indonesia : Sense Sensibility* (Part III of a Symposium on Afro-Asia's intellectuals), The New Leader, June 6, 1960, pp. 19-22.

——. *Agricultural Involution : The Process of Ecological Change*

in Indonesia, Berkeley, University of California Press, 1963.
Geertz C.J, Jr. : *Peddlers and Princes : Social development and economic change in two Indonesian towns*, Chicago, The University of Chicago Press, 1963.

Ghurey, G.S. : "The Teaching of Sociology, Social Psychology and Social Anthropology" in *The Teaching of Social Sciences in India*, UNESCO Publications, 1956.

Goldschmidt, Walter : "An Ethnography of Encounters : A Methodology for the enquiry into the Relation between the individual and Society", *Current Anthropology*, vol. 13, No. 1, 1972, pp. 59-78.

——. On "Comparative Functionalism" in *Newsletter of the American Anthropological Association*. vol. 15, No. 6, 1974, pp. 21-22.

Gore, M.S. : *America and Social Science in India*, n.d.

Gorer, G. : "Themes in Japanese Culture" in *Transactions of New York Academy of Sciences*, Series II, vol. 5, 1943, pp. 106-124.

Gorer, G. and M. Mead : *Balinese Character : A Photographic Analysis*; Special Publication of New York Academy of Science, 1942.

Gorer, G. and J. Rickman : *The People of Great Russia*, London, Cresset, 1949.

Goswami, P.D. : *Ballads and Tales of Assam* (A study of folklore of Assam), Gauhati, University of Gauhati, 1960.

Gough, E.K. : "The Nayar Tarawad", *Journal of M.S. University of Baroda*, 1(2), 1952, pp. 1-13.

——. "Incest Prohibitions and Rules of Exogamy in Three Matrilineal Groups of the Malabar Coast", *International Archives of Ethnography*, vol. 26, 1952.

——. "Changing Kinship Usages in the setting of Political and Economy Change Among the Nayars of Malabar", *Journal of Royal Anthropological Institute*, vol. 82, Part I, 1952, pp. 71-88.

Greetz, Clifford : "Religion as a Cultural System" in Clifford Greetz, *The Interpretation of Culture*, New York, Basic Books, 1973.

Handoo, Jawaharlal : "Levi-Strauss and Structural Folkloristics" in *International journal of Dravidian Linguistics*, vol. 5, No. 1, 1976, pp. 86-107.

Hanks, L.M. : "Culture of the Central Thai" in *Ethnic group of Mainland South-east Asia*, Edited by F.M. Lebard, G.C. Hickey, and J.S. Musgrave, New Haven, Human Relations Area Files Press, 1954.

Hanks, L.M. and M. Phillip : "A Young Thai from the countryside" in *Studying Personality Cross Cultural* ed. B. Kaplan Evanston, Raw Peterson, 1961, pp. 637-656.

Harper, Edward B. : *Religion in South Asia*, Scattle, University of Washington Press, 1964.

Harris, Marvin : *The Rise of Anthropological Theories*, London, Routledge and Kegan Paul, 1968.

Hatanaka, Sachiko : "The Changing Culture of Newly Contacted People in the Highland of New Guinea" in *Proceedings of the VIIIth ICAES* vol. II, Tokyo & Kyoto, Science Council of Japan, 1968, pp. 170-71.

Heine-Geldern Robert : "Die asiatische Herkunft der Sudamerikanischen Metalltechnik" in *Paideuma*, vol. 5, 1954, pp. 347-423.

——. "Das Problem Vorkolumbischer Beziehum gen Zwischen Alter and Neuer Welt und Seine Bedeutung far die allgemeine Kulturgeschichte" in *Anzeiger der Osterreichischen Akademic der Wissen Schuften, Philos-histor*, Klasse, vol. 91, No. 24, 1954, pp. 343-357.

Herskovits, Melville J. : *Cultural Anthropology*, New York, 1955.

——. "Some Further Comments on Cultural Relativism", *American Anthropologist*, vol. 60, No. 2, 1958, pp. 266-273.

Hitchcock, John T. : *The Magars of Banyan Hill*, London, Holt, Rinchart and Winston, 1966.

Hodgen, Margaret T. : "Similarities and dates distribution", in *American Anthropologist*, vol. 52, No. 4, Part I, 1950, pp. 445-468.

——. *Change and History* (Viking Fund Publications in Anthropology No. 18), New York, Wenner-Gren Foundation for Anthropological Research Inc., 1952.

Hofer, Tomas : "Anthropology and Native Ethnographers in Central European Villages : Comparative Notes on the Professional Personality of two Disciplines", *Current Anthropology*, vol. 9, No. 4, 1968, pp. 311-315.

Honigmann, John J. : *The Development of Anthropological Ideas*, Homewood, Illinois, The Dorsey Press, 1976.

Hooykaas, C. : "Bauddha Brahmins in Bali", *Bulletin of School Oriental and African Studies*, 26, 1963, pp. 544-550.

——. *Agana Tirtha, Fine Studies in Hindu Balinese religion*, Royal Dutch Academy North Holland Publishing Co., 1964.

Horvath, Ronald J. : "A Definition of Colonialism", *Current Anthropology*, vol. 13, No. 1, 1972, pp. 45-58.

Howard, B.D. : *Life with Trans-Siberian Savages*, London, Longmans, Green, 1893.

Hsu, Francis L.K. : "*Caste, Clan and Club*", Princeton, New Jersey, D. Van' No Strand Company Inc., 1963.

Hultkrantz, Ake : *General Ethnological Concepts*, Copenhagen, Rosenkilde and Bagger, 1960.

——. "Anthropology as a goal of Research : Some Reflexions", *Folk*, 7, 1965, pp. 5-22.

——. "Some Remarks on Contemporary European Ethnological thought"; *Ethnologia Europea*, I, 1967, pp. 38-44.

——. "The Aims of Anthropology : A Scandinavian Point of View", *Current Anthropology*, vol. 9, No. 4, 1968, pp. 289-310.

Hunt, C.L. : "Americanisation Process in the Philippines", *Indian Quarterly* 12, 1956, pp. 118-130.

Hunt, C.L. with S. Espiritu : *Community development : The Phillippine Story*, Manila, Garcia, 1964.

Hutton, J.H. : *Census of India, vol. I, India Part III B, Ethnographic Notes*, Simla, Government of India Press, 1931.

ICSSR (ed.) : *A Survey of Reserch in Sociology and Social Anthropology*, vol. III, Bombay, Popular Prakashan, 1972.

——. *A Survey of Reseach in Sociology and Social Anthropology*, vol. II, Bombay, Popular Prakashan, 1974.

Ikram, S.M. and Percival Spear : *The Cultural Heritage of Pakistan*, London, Oxford University Press, 1955.

Ishida, E : On the "Problem of Process : Results on Anthropology as a Field of Study and on Values" in Sol Tax, ed., *An Appraisal of Anthropology Today*, Chicago, The University of Chicago Press, 1953.

——. "Urbanization and its Impact on Japanese Politics", Presented in the *Meetings of I.S.A. Research Committee on*

Urban Sociology at 6th World Congress of Sociology, at Evian, 1966.

Ismagilova, R.N. : "TheE thnic Factors in Modern Africa" in I.R. Grigulevich and S.Y. Kozlov (eds.), *Races and Peoples: Contemporary Ethnic and Racial Problems*, Moscow, Progress Publishers, 1974, pp. 212-256.

Itawa, K. : "Ritual Symbols in the northern part of South-east Asia", *Nature and Life in South-east Asia*, 4, 1965.

Ivanicek, F. : On "Anthropology as a Field of Study" in Sol Tax et al (eds.), *An Appraisal of Anthropology Today*, Chicago, University of Chicago Press, 1953.

Iwata, K. : *Minority groups in Northern Laos especially the Yao Laos Project*, Paper No. 18, Los Angeles, University of California Press, 1959.

——. "The Process of disorganisation and re-organisation of rural society in Northern Thailand (in Japanese)", *Journal of South-east Asian Studies*, 2(2), 1964.

Jain, R.K. : *South Indian on the Plantation Frontier in Malaya*, New Haven and London, Yale University Press, 1970.

——. "Main Present Trends of Social Cultural Anthropological Researches in India and Pakistan" in *UNESCO International Study of Main Trends of Research in the Social and Human Sciences*, UNESCO, MSS, 1971.

Jay, Edward J. : "*A Tribal Village of Middle India*", Calcutta, Anthropological Survey of India, 1970.

——. "The Anthropologist and Tribal Welfare : Hill Maria : A Case Study", *Journal of Social Research*, vol. XI, No. 2, 1959, pp. 82-89.

Jha, M. : *Sacred Complex in Janakpur*, Allahabad, United Publishers, 1971

Joel, C.E. : "The New Diffusionist, (A Study of Inter-Relationships in Cultural Anthropology)" in *Quarterly*, No. 3, 1971.

Jones, W.T. : "World Views : Their nature and their function", *Current Anthropology*, vol. 13, No. 1, 1972, pp. 79-109.

Judd, L.C. : *Tong Taa Village*, (Unpublished M.S. Thesis), New York, Cornel University, Ithaca, 1954.

Kardinar, A. : *The Individual and his Society*, New York, Columbia University Press, 1939 (ed.).

Kardinar, A. et al. : *The Psychological Frontiers of Society*, New York, Columbia University Press, 1945.

Karim, A.K. Nazunul : *Changing Society in India and Pakistan: A Story in Social change and Social Stratification*, Dacca, Geoffery Cumberlege, Oxford University Press, 1945.

Karve, Irwati : *Kinship Organisatian in India*, Poona, Deccan College Research Institute (also published from Asia Publishing House, Bombay), 1953.

Kaufman, H.K. : *Bangkhuad*, North Carolina, Augustine Press, 1962.

——. *Cu Lao—a finishing Village and its co-operative*, Ministry of Agriculture, Saigon, 1963.

Kickert, R.W. : "A Pilot Village Study in Northeastern Thailand" in *U.S. Information Service Report*, No. 3, 1960.

Kikuchi, L.Y. : Family and Society of Filipino majority groups (in Japanese), *Studies in Archaic Culture of China*, 2, 1965.

Kluckhohn, Clyde, Henry A. Murray & David M. Schneider : *Personality in Nature, Society and Culture*, New York, Alfred A. Knoff, 1953.

Koppers, W. : *Primitive Man and His World Picture*, London, New York, Sheed and Ward, 1952.

——. "Diffusion : Transmission and Acceptance" in William L. Thomas Jr. (ed.) *Current Anthropology, A Supplement to Anthropology Today*, Chicago, The University of Chicago Press, 1956.

Kroeber, A.L. : "Classificatory System of Relationship", *Journal of Royal Anthropological Institute of Great Britain* and *Ireland*, vol. 39, 1909, pp. 77-84.

——. "*Culture and Natural Areas of Native North America*", University of California, Publications in American Archaeology and Ethnology, vol. 38, 1939.

——. *Anthropology Today*, Chicago, Illinois, The University of Chicago Press, (ed.), 1953.

——. "Introduction" to his edited volume *Anthropology Today*, Ibid, 1953.

——. "History of Anthropological Thought" in *Current Anthropology : A Supplement to Anthropology Today*, ed. William Thomas, Jr., Chicago, The University of Chicago Press, 1956, pp. 293-311.

——. *An Anthropologist Looks at History*, Berkeley, University of California Press, 1963.

Kudryavtsev, M.K. : *Community and Caste in Hindustan* (Indian Village), Moscow, 1971.

Lehman, F.K. : *The Structure of Chin Society : A Tribal People adapted to a non-western Civilization*, Illinois, Anthropology Series No. 3, 1963.

Leade, Walfgang : "Urgent Anthropology : Ethnological Research Needs in Oceania", *Current Anthropology*, vol. II, Nos. 4-5, 1970, pp. 475-476.

Lee, D. : "Folk Beliefs of Sacred Poles in Korea" in *Proceedings of VIIIth ICAES*, vol. II, Tokyo & Kyoto, Science Council of Japan, 1968, pp. 68-70.

Lebar, F.M. et al. : *Ethnic groups of Mainland South-east Asia*, New Haven, HRAF Press, 1964.

Lewis, Oscar : *Group Dynamics in a North Indian Village*, Delhi Planning Commission, 1954.

Levin, M.G. : "*Origin and Migration of the Indo-Aryans*", Firma K.L. Mukhopadhyay, Calcutta, 1972.

Levi-Strauss, C. : "Structural Analysis in Linguistics and in Anthropology" in Levi-Strauss, *Structural Anthropology*, trans. Claire Jacebson and Brooke Grundfest Scheept, New York, Basic Book, 1944 (Org.).

——. On the "Social Science and Anthropology" in *An Appraisal of Anthropology Today* (eds.) Sol Tax et al, Chicago, The University of Chicago Press, 1953.

——. On the "Problems of the Historical Approach : Results" in Sol Tax ed. *An Appraisal of Anthropology Today*, Chicago, The University of Chicago Press, 1953.

——. *Totemism* (trans. Rodney Needham), Boston, Beacon Press, 1963.

——. "Anthropology : Its Achievement and Future", *Current Anthropology*, vol. 7, No. 2, 1966.

Leiban, R.W. : "Shamanism and Social Control in a Philippine City", *Journal of the Folklore Institute*, 1965.

Little, K. : "The Content of Social Change", *American Anthropological Association, Memoir*, No. 144, 1963.

Linton, R. : *The Cultural Background of Personality*, New York, Appleton Century Crofts, 1945.

Loffler, L.G. : "Carrying Capacity, Schwenbhan Problem in Sudostasien", *Acts du Vle Congress International des Sciences Anthropologists*, vol. 2(1), 1963, pp. 179-82.

Lowie, R.H. : *History of Ethnological Theory*, New York, Farrar and Renchart, 1937.

——. *Social Organisation*, London, Routledge and Kegan Paul Ltd., 1950.

——. On the "Problems of the Historical Approach : Theory" in Sol Tax ed. *An Appraisal of Anthropology Today*, Chicago, The University of Chicago Press, 1953.

Madan, T.N. : *Family and Kinship : A Study of the Pandits of Rural Kashmir*, Bombay, Asia Publishing House, 1965.

——. "Political Pressures and Ethnical constraints upon Indian Sociologists" in Gideon Sjoberg (ed.) *Ethnic Politics and Social Research*, Cambridge, Massachusetts, Schenloman Publishing Company Inc., 1967, pp. 162-179.

Maday, Bela C. : "Hungarian Anthropology : The Problem of Communication", *Current Anthropology*, vol. 9, Nos. 2-3, 1968, pp. 180-184.

Majumdar, D.N.: "Bongaism" in *Essay in Anthropology presented to Rai Bahadur S.C. Roy*, ed. by J.P. Mills and Others, Lucknow, Maxwell & Co., 1942.

——. "The Changing Canvas of Tribal Life", *Eastern Anthropologist*, vol. 14, No. 1, 1949.

——. "Anthropology Under Glass", *The Journal of Anthropological Society of Bombay*, 1950.

——. *The Affairs of Tribe : A Study in Tribal Dynamics*, Lucknow, The Universal Publishers Ltd., 1950.

——. "Introduction" in D.N. Majumdar (ed.) *Rural Profiles*, Lucknow, Ethnographic and Folk Culture Society, U.P., 1955.

——. "Special Report on the Teaching of Social Anthropology" in *The Teaching of Social Sciences in India*, UNESCO Publication, 1956.

——. *Caste and Communication in an Indian Village*, Bombay, Asia Publishing House, 1958.

——. *The Himalayan Polyandry*, Bombay, Asia Publishing House, 1962.

Mandelbaum, David G. : *Society in India* (two vols.), Bombay, Popular Prakashan, 1972.

Manndorff, H. : *Report on the Socio-economic Survey of the Hill Tribes in Northern Thailand*, Department Public Welfare,

Ministry of Interior, Bangkok, Thailand (Revised Version in Press).

Manndorff, H. : "Problems bei der Einfuhrung d. Staatlichen Verwaltung unter den Bergstammch von Nordthailand", *Sociologus* 13(1), 1963, pp. 15-31.

——. "Socio-economic research in support of Socio-economic development in the Hill Tribe Project in Northern Thailand", *Journal of the Public Welfare Department*, 9(4), 1964.

Mannheim, Karl : *Diagnosis of Our Time*, London, 1943.

——. *Systematic Sociology*, London, 1957.

Maretin, Y.V. : On "Indonesia", MSS. Presented in the *VIIIth ICAES*, Moscow, 1964.

Mathur, K.S. : *Caste and Ritual in a Malwa Village*, Bombay, Asia Publishing House, 1964.

Matsumoto, N. : "An introduction to the Study of Indo-China (in Japanese), *Japanese Journal of Ethnology*, 23(1-2), 1959, p. 3.

——. Indo-Chinese Studies (in Japanese), Yokohama, 1965.

Mayer, A.C. : *Caste and Kinship in Central India : A Village and its Region*, London, Routledge and Kegan Paul, 1960.

McCarthy, Frederick D. : "The Oceanic and Indonesian Affiliations of Australian : A Aborigional Culture", *The Journal of the Polynesian Society*, vol. 62, No. 3, 1953, pp. 243-261.

McVey, R.T. : *Indonesia* (ed.), New Haven, Human Relations Area Files Press, 1963.

Mead, M. : *Coming of Age in Samoa*, New York, Morrow, 1928.

——*Growing up in New Guinea*, New York, Blue Ribbon, 1930.

——. *Sex and Temperament in Three Primitive Societies*, New York, Morrow, 1935.

——. *Co-operation and Competition among Primitive Peoples*, New York, McGraw-Hill, 1937.

——. *Male and Female*, New York, Morrow, 1949.

——. "The Study of National Character" in D. Lerner and H.D. Haswell eds., *The Policy Sciences*, Standard, Standard University Press, 1951.

——. On the "Social Science and Anthropology" in *An Appraisal of Anthropology Today* (eds.) Sol Tax et. al, Chicago, Illinois, The University of Chicago Press, 1953.

Mead, M. : *New Lives for the Old*, New York, William Morrow and Company, 1956.

Mencher, Joan P. : "Changing Familial Roles among South Malabar Nayers", in *South Eastern Journal of Anthropology*, 18(3), 1962, pp. 230-246.

Mendelson, E.M. : "Religion and Authority in Modern Burma", *The World Today*, vol. 16, No. 3, 1960, pp. 110-118.

——. "The Uses of Religious Scepticism in Modern Burma", *Diogenes*, 1963, p.44.

——. "Buddhism and the Burmese establishment", *Archives de Sociologies des Religions*, vol. 9, No. 17, 1964, pp. 85-95.

Menden, F.R. von Der : *Religion and nationalism in Southeast Asia*, Madison, University of Wisconsin Press, 1963.

Mukherjee, R.K. : *Family in India : A Perspective*, Calcutta, Indian Statistical Ins., 1969.

Murdock, G.P. : *Social Structure*, New York, Macmillan & Co., 1949.

Murphy, Gardner : *In the Minds of Men : The Study of Human Behaviour and Social Tensions in India*, New York, Basic Books, Inc. Publishers, 1955.

Naik, T.B. : "Applied Anthropology in India" in *A survey of Research in Sociology and Social Anthropology*, vol. III, by ICSSR, Bombay, Popular Prakashan, 1972.

Naken, Chie : "A Plural Society in Sikkim—A Study of the Interrelations of Lepchas, Bhotias and Nepalis" in C. Von Furer-Haimendrof ed. *Caste and kin in Nepal, India and Ceylon : Anthropological Studies in Hindu Buddhist Contact Zones*, Bombay, Asia Publishing House, 1966, pp. 213-263.

——. *Garo and Khasi : A Comparative Study of Matrilineal Systems*, Paris and the Hague, Mouton & Co., 1967.

——. *Kinship and Economic Organisation in Rural Japan*, London, Athlone Press, 1967.

——. *Tateshakai no Nigen Kankei* (Personal Relations in a vertical Society), Tokyo, Kodansha, 1967.

——. *Garo and Khasi : A Comparative Study in Matrilineal System*, Paris, Monton & Co., 1968.

—— : *Japanese Society*, London, Weidenfield & Nicolson & Berkeley, University of California Press, 1970.

——. *Human Relations in Japan*, Tokyo, Ministry of Foreign Affairs, Japan, 1972.

Namba, Monkichi : *Japanese Translation : Concept of Culture* (by Clyde Kluchkhohn), Sogensha, Osaka, 1948.

——. *Japanese Translation : Social Anthropology* (by Evanspritchard), Tokyo, Dohunkan, 1957.

Narayan, Jaiprakash : "Gandhism and Social Sciences", *AVARD Newsletter*, vol. VI, No. 5, September-October, 1964.

Nash, J. : "Living with Nats : An Analysis of Spirit animism" in *Anthropological Studies in Theravada Buddhism, Southeast Asia Studies*, Yale University, 1966.

——. "Burmese Buddhism in everyday life," *American Anthropologist*, 65, 1963, pp. 285-295.

Nash, M. : "Southeast Asian Society : Dual or multiple," *Journal of Asian Studies*, 23, 1964, pp. 417-23.

Needham, R. : "A note on some North Borneo kinship terminologies", *Journal Malayam Branch, Royal Asiatic Society*, 26, 1953, pp, 221-223.

Nepali, G.S. : *The Newars : An Ethno-Sociological Study of a Himalayan Community*, Bombay, United Asia Publications, 1965.

Ness, G.D. : *Trends report on Social Stratification and Social mobility in Malaya*, UNESCO (Tokyo), East Asia Cultural Studies, 1965.

Newsletter : *Fulbright Newsletter*, New Delhi, U.S. Educational Foundation in India, 1964.

——. "*Fellow Newsletter*" *American Anthropological Association*, vol. 8, No. 4, Correspondence, 1967.

Niitsu, Koichi : "Processual Change of Rural to Urban Value : A Cross-Cultural Study of Asian Students coming from Rural Areas" in *Proceedings of VIIIth ICAES*, Tokyo and Kyoto, Science Council of Japan, 1968, pp. 134-138.

Obayashi, T. : "The Lawa and Sgan Karen in North-Western Thailand", *Journal of the Siam Society* 52, 1964, pp. 199-216.

Pehroson, Robert N. : *The Social Origanisation of the Marri Baluck*, Chicago, Aldine Publishing Company, 1966.

Piers, Ralph (ed.) : *Traditional Sinhalese Culture : A Symposium*, Peradeniya, Ceylon University Conference on Traditional Culture, 1956.

Pike, Kenneth : *Language in Relation to a Unified Theory of the Structure of Human Behaviour*, vol. I, Glendale, Summer Institute of Linguistics, 1954.

Puckkov, P.I. : "Ethnic Processes in Oceania" in I. R. Grigulevich and S.Y. Kozlov (eds.) *Races and Peoples : Contemporary Ethnic and Racial Problems*, Moscow, Progress Publishers, 1974, pp. 257-274.

Radcliffe-Brown, A.R. : *The Andaman Islanders : A Study in Social Anthropology*, The Free Press, Glence, Illinois, 1922.

——. "The Study of Kinship System", *Journal of Royal Anthropological Institute*, vol. 71, 1941, pp. 1-18.

——. "Introduction" in A.R. Radcliffe-Brown and Daryll Forde (eds.) in *African System of Kinship and Marriage*, London, Oxford University Press, 1950.

——. *Structure and Function in Primitive Society*, London, Cohen & West Ltd., 1952.

——. *An Appraisal of Anthropology Today*, Chicago, The University of Chicago Press, 1953.

——. *The Natural Science of Society*, Glence, Illinois, the Free Press, 1957 (1948 MSS).

Redfield, Robert : *The Primitive World and its Transformation*, Ithaca, New York, Cornell University Press, 1953.

——. *The Little Community (view points for the study of a Human whole)*, Chicago, The University of Chicago Press, 1955.

Report; Motoami, J. et.al : *Nationality of the Japanese*, Tokyo, Shisei-Scobr, 1961.

Risley, R.H., Gait, E.A. : *Census of India, 1901*, vol. I, Culcutta, Government of India, 1903.

Rivers, W.H.R. : *The Todas*, London, Macmillan & Co., 1906.

Rosser, Colin : Social Mobility in the Newar Caste System" in C. von Furer-Haimendorf (ed.) *Caste and Kin in Nepal, India and Ceylon*, Bombay, Asia Publishing House, 1966, pp. 68-139.

Roy Burman, B.K. : *A Second Look at Tribal Ethnography of India*, MSS, New Delhi, Social Studies Unit, Census Operation, 1977.

Roy, S.C. : "Researches in Anthropology in India," *Man in India*, vol. II, 1922.

Rubin, V.A. : *On Eastern Asia*, MSS, Presented in the VIIth ICAES, Moscow, 1964.

Rupp, Britter (ed.) : *International Bibliography in Social Sciences, Anthropology*, vol. XX, 1974, London, Tavistock Publications Ltd., 1976.

Ryan, Bryce and others : "*Sinhalese Village*," Florida, University of Miami Press, 1958.

Saran, Gopala and D.P. Sinha : "Status of Social-cultural Anthropology in India," *Annual Review Anthropology*, vol. 5, UNESCO, Paris, 1976.

Saraswati, B.N.: *Kashi : Myth and Reality of a Classical Cultural Tradition*, Simla, Indian Institute of Advanced Study, 1976.

Sargent, S.S. and M.W. Smith (eds.) : *Culture and Personality*, New York, Wenner Gren Foundation for Anthropological Research Inc., 1949.

Schneider, David M. : *American Kinship : A Cultural Account*, Englewodd Cliffs, N.J., Printice-Hall, 1968.

Schuster, Carl : "The Ainu Inao : Some comparative considerations" in *Proceedings of VIIIth ICAES*, 1968, pp. 86-98.

Seligmann, G.G. and B.G. Seligmann : *The Veddas of Ceylon*, Cambridge University Press, 1911.

Sengupta, Shankar : *Folklore Researches in India*, Culcutta, Indian Publication, 1964

Service, Elman R. : *Primitive Social Organisation*, New York, Bandom House, 1962.

Shiratori, Y. : "Classification of Substance type of the Ethnic Groups of South and South-western China" presented in *The Folklore and Ethno-musicology Division*, Anthropology Section (X) of 11th Pacific Science Congress, Tokyo, 1966.

——. "The Genealogy of Ethnic Groups in Southern China—Historical Note" in *Proceedings of VIIIth ICAES*, vol. II, Tokyo and Kyoto, Science Council of Japan, 1968, p. 67.

Singer, M. and B.S. Cohn (eds.) : *Structure and Change in Indian Society*, Chicago, Aldine Publishing Company, 1968.

Singh, K.S. (ed.) : *Tribal Situation in India*, Simla, Indian Institute of Advanced Study, 1972.

Sinha, Purnima and D.P. Sinha : "Alfred Louis Kroeber : His contributions to Anthropological theory," *Anthropos*, vol. 63-64, 1968-69, pp. 793-807.

Sinha, S.C. : "Is there an Indian Tradition in Social Culture Anthropology : Retrospect and Prospect" in *Abstract Conference on the Nature and Function of Anthropological*

Traditions, Wenner Gren Foundation for Anthropological Research, New York, 1968.

Sinha, S.C. : "Is there an Indian Tradition in Social/Cultural Anthropology : Retrospect and Prospect," *Journal of Indian Anthropological Society*, vol. 6, pp. 1-14., 1971.

Sjoberg, G. : *Ethics, Politics and Social Research* (ed.), Cambridge, Schenkman Publishing Company Inc. 1967

Skinner, G.W. : *Report on the universe in South-East Asia*, Data paper No. 1, South-East Asia Program, Cornell University, 1951.

——. *Chinese Society in Thailand*: *An Analytical History*, Ithaca, Cornell University Press, 1957.

——. *Editor, Local Ethnic and National Loyalities in Village Indonesia* : *A Symposium*, South-East Asia Studies, Yale University, 1959.

——. "The Thailand Chinese : Assimilation in a Changing Society," *Asia*, vol. 2, 1964, pp. 80-92.

Soejono, R.P. : "Preliminary Notes on new finds of Lower-Palaeolithic implements from Indonesia," *Asian Perspectives*, 5, 1961, pp. 217-232.

Solenberger, Robert R. : "Cultural Conflict and Language Learning in Micronesia" in *Proceedings of VIIIth ICAES*, vol. II, Tokyo and Kyoto, Science Council of Japan, 1968, pp. 364-367.

Sopher, D.E. : "Population Dislocation in the Chittagong Hills", *Geographical Review*, 53, 1963, pp. 337-362.

——. "The Swidden Wetrice transition Zone in the Chittagong Hills", *Annals of the Association of American Geographers*, 54, 1964, pp. 107-126.

Spiro, Melford E. : *Burmese Supernaturalism*, Englewood Cliffs, N.J., Prentice-Hall, 1967.

——. "An over view and a Suggested Reorientation" in Francis L.K. Hsu ed. *Psychological Anthropology*, new ed., Cambridge, Schenkman Publication Co., 1972.

Sriniwas, M.N. : *Religion and Society*; *Among the Coorgs of South India*, Bombay, Oxford University Press, 1952.

——. *India's Village*, Calcutta, Asia Publishing House, 1955.

Steward, Julian : *Theory of Culture Change*, Urbana, University of Illinois Press, 1955.

Stone, R. : "Inter-group relations Among the Taosung, Samar and Badjan of Sulu", *Philippine Sociological Review*, 10 (3), 1962, p.4.

——. *Some Comments on Muslim Social Organization*, Institute of Philippine Literature, In Press.

Sturtevant, W. : "Studies in Ethnoscience", *American Anthropologist*, vol. 66, Part 2, 1964, pp. 99-131.

Suenari, Michio : "Affinal relationships among the Puyuma of Taiwan" in *Proceedings of VIIIth ICAES*, vol. II, Tokyo and Kyoto, Science Council of Japan, 1968, pp. 134-138.

Sumiya, Mikio : "Christianity and the Formation of Modern Japan", *VIIIth ICAES*, Tokyo, Science Council of Japan, 1968 MSS.

Swift, M.G. : "Malayan Politics", *Race and class civilisation*, 12 (2), 1962.

——. "The Status of Malay Women" in *Women of the New Asia*, edited by B. Ward, 1964.

——. "*Malay Peasant Society in Jelebu*", London School of Economics Monographs on Social Anthropology, No. 29, 1965.

Tambiah, S.J. : "Polyandry in Ceylon—with special reference to the Leggala Region" in *Caste aud Kin in Nepal, India and Ceylon* (ed.) C. von Furer-Haimendorf, Bombay, Asia Publishing House, 1966, pp. 264-358.

Tax, Sol et.al (eds.) : *An Appraisal of Anthropology Today*, Chicago, The University of Chicago Press, 1953.

——. "Action Anthropology," *Journal of Social Research*, Vol. II, 1959.

——. "Action Anthropology", *Applied Anthropology in India* (ed.) L.P. Vidyarthi, Allahabad, Kitab Mahal, 1968.

——. "General Editor's Preface" in Paul Hockings, ed., *Principles of Visual Anthropology*, The Hague, Mouton Publishers, 1975.

——. "*Fifth International Directoy of Anthropologists*", ed. Current Anthropology Resource Series, Chicago, The University of Chicago Press, 1975.

Thakur, U.T. : *Sindhi Culture*, Bombay, University of Bombay, 1959.

Thomas, William L. (ed.) : *Current Anthropology (Supplement to Anthropology Today*), Chicago, The University of Chicago Press, 1956.

Thompson, Laura : *Towards a Science of Mankind*, New York, McGraw-Hill Book Co., 1961.

Thompson, L.C. : "Saigon Phonemics" in *Language*, 35, 1959, pp. 454-476.

Tiger, Lionel : *Men in Groups*, London, Nelson, 1970.

Tiger, Lionel and Robind Fox : *The Imperial Animal*, New York, Dell Publishing Co., 1971.

Tugby, D.J. : "Ethnological and Allied work on South-east Asia, 1950-66", *Current Anthropology*, vol. 9, Nos. 2-3, 1968, pp. 185-206.

Tugby, Elise : "The Distribution of Ethnological and Allied Field work in South-East Asia, 1950-66", *Current Anthropology*, vol. 9, Nos. 2-3, 1968, pp. 207-213.

Turner, Victor W. : "*The Forest of Symbols*", Leiden, E.J. Brill, 1967.

Upadhyay, K.D. : *Lok Sahitya ki Bhumika*, Allahabad, Sahitya Bhavan Pvt. Ltd., 1957.

U.S.E.F.I. : *Directory of Fulbright Grantees*, New Delhi, The United States Educational Foundation in India, 1964.

Vidyarthi, L.P. : "Anthropology, Authority and Tribal Welfare in India", *Eastern Anthropologist*, vol. XI, No. 1, 1957.

——. *Indian Anthropology in Action* (ed.), Ranchi, Council of Social and Cultural Research, Bihar, 1960.

——. *The Sacred Complex of Hindu Gaya*, Bombay, Asia Publishing House, 1961.

——. *Aspects of Religion in Indian Society*, Meerut, Kedarnath Ramnath, 1962 (ed.)

——. *The Maler : A Study in Nature-Man-Spirit Complex of a Hill Tribe*, Calcutta, Bookland Pvt. Ltd., 1963.

——. Social-Anthropological Researches in India : Some preliminary Observations", *Journal of Social Research*, vol. IX, No. 1, 1966, pp. 1-74.

——. "Social Sciences in India : A Social Anthropological Approach", *Social Science Information*, Vol. V, UNESCO, Paris, 1966.

——. *Leadership in India* (ed.), Bombay, Asia Publishing Co., 1967.

Vidyarthi, L.P. : *Applied Anthropology in India* (ed.), Allahabad, Kitab Mahal, 1968.

——. "Psycho-Anthropological Researches in India", *Journal of Social Research*, vol. XII, No. 2, 1969.

——. *Conflict, Tension and Social change in Contemporary India* (ed.), Calcutta, Punthi Pustak, 1969.

——. *Cultural Configuration of Ranchi*, (a Survey) New Delhi, Planning Commission, Government of India, Distributor : Council of Social and Cultural Research, Bihar, Ranchi, 1969.

——. *Socio-Cultural Implications of Industrialization in India : Tribal Bihar, A Case Study*, New Delhi, Planning Commission, Government of India, Distributor : Council of Social and Cultural Research, Bihar, Ranchi, 1970.

——. *Folklore Researches in India*, Calcutta, Indian Publication, 1974 (ed.)

——. *The Dynamics of Tribal Leadership in Bihar* (with K.N. Sahay), Allahabad, Kitab Mahal, 1976.

——. "Applied Anthropology in India" in *Anthropology in India*, vol. I, Cultural Anthropology (ed.) S.C. Sinha, Calcutta, Anthropological Survey of India, 1976, pp. 81-116.

——. *Rise of Social Anthropology in India*, 2 vols., Delhi, Concept Publishing Company, 1977.

Vidyarthi, L.P. & B.K. Rai : *The Tribal Culture of India*, Delhi, Concept Publishing Company, 1977.

Vidyarthi, L.P. & M. Jha (ed.) : *Sacred Complex in India*, Ranchi, Council of Social & Cultural Research, Bihar, 1974.

Wallace, A.F.C. : "Mental Illness, Biology and Culture" in Hsu, *Psychological Anthropology*, Homewood, Illinois, Dorsey Press, 1961.

——. "The Problem of Psychological Validity of Componential Analysis", *American Anthropologist*, Vol. 67, No. 5, Part 2, 1965, pp. 229-248.

——. *Culture and Personality* (2nd ed.), New York, Random House, 1970.

Wallce, A.F.C. & John Atkins : "The Meaning of Kinship Terms", *American Anthropologist*, vol. 62, 1960, pp. 54-80.

Wallmott, W.E. : *The Chinese in Cambodia*, Vancouver, University of British Columbia Press, In Press.

Ward, Robert E. : "Japan : The Continuity of Modernization" in *Political Culture and Political Development*, ed. by Lucian W. Pye and Sidney Verba, Princeton, 1965.

White, Leslie A. : *The Science of Culture*, New York, Grove Press, 1949.

Whiting, John W.M. & Irvin L. Child : *Child Training and Personality : A Cross-Cultural Study*, New Haven, Yale University Press, 1953.

Wiser, W.H. : *The Hindu jajmani System*, Lucknow, Lucknow Publishing House, 1936.

Wissler, C. : *The American Indian : An Introduction to the Anthropology of the New World*, New York, D.C. Mc-Murtrie, 1917.

Zaidi, S.M. Hafeez : *The Village Culture in Transition : A study of East Pakistan Rural Society*, Honolulu, East-West Centre Press, 1970.

Index